More Water into Wine

More Water into Wine

Helen Brown

Reading Stones Publishing

Copyright © 2020 by Helen Brown.

ISBN: Softcover: 978-0-6488143-8-2
        eBook: 978-0-6488143-9-9

All rights reserved. No part of this book may be reproduced or transmitted in any form or by any means, electronic or mechanical, including photocopying, recording, or by any information storage and retrieval system, without permission in writing from the copyright owner.

Scripture quotations marked KJV are from the Holy Bible, King James Version (Authorized Version). First published in 1611. Quoted from the KJV Classic Reference Bible, Copyright © 1983 by The Zondervan Corporation.

Scripture quotations marked WEB are from the Holy Bible, World English Bible obtained from www.biblegateway.com

Any people depicted in stock imagery provided by Shutterstock are models, and such images are being used for illustrative purposes only. www.shutterstock.com

Special thanks to Anne Webster for allowing us to photograph her fountain.

Cover photo and cover design: Wendy Wood

Published by: Reading Stones Publishing
Helen Brown and Wendy Wood
hbrown19561@gmail.com
woodwendy1982.wixsite.com/readingstones

To order additional copies of this book contact the publisher at:
Glenburnie homestead
212 Glenburnie Rd
Rob Roy NSW 2360
hbrown19561@gmail.com

CONTENTS

1. A Start	1
2. A Wheel Bearing	2
3. A Blessed Day	3
4. A Conversation	4
5. A Day to Forget	5
6. A Few More Steps	6
7. A Good Mechanic	7
8. A Light at the end of a Tunnel	8
9. A Torch Beam	9
10. A Wonderful Teacher	10
11. Battle Weary	11
12. Being Winners	12
13. Caring	13
14. Christmas Night	14
15. Clang, Clang, Clang	15
16. Clear Vision	16
17. Coming Home	17
18. Crying Out	19
19. Damaged	20
20. Death, Jail or Jesus	21
21. Depression and Bullies; Part 1	22
22. Depression and Bullies; Part 2	23
23. Different Angle	25
24. Don't judge a book by its cover	26
25. Dreams and Plans	27
26. Easter Sunday – We Celebrate	29
27. Eating Right	30
28. Equality of Men and Women	31
29. Far from Home	33
30. Farmer's Friends	34
31. Feeling Important	35
32. Focus	36
33. Fog	37

34. Giving or Receiving	38
35. God Doesn't Need Me	39
36. God's Garden	40
37. God's light	41
38. God's Timing	42
39. Greatness	43
40. Growing in the Dark	44
41. Have I Done Enough?	45
42. Heaven is a Real Place	46
43. Here We Go Again	47
44. Ignorance is Bliss?	48
45. International Day for Women	49
46. Jigsaw	51
47. Know what we ask for!	52
48. Kookaburra Sing	53
49. Left Behind	54
50. Lessons from my Woodbox - Matthew 22:1-10	55
51. Let Go and Let God	57
52. Letting Go	58
53. Life Giving Water	59
54. Life's Road	60
55. Life's Storybook	61
56. Light Bulb Moments	62
57. Looking a Gift Horse in the Mouth	63
58. Looking Back	64
59. Loudly Proclaim	65
60. Loving Us	67
61. Makeover	68
62. Missed Opportunities	69
63. Missing Ingredient	71
64. Mobile Phones and the Bible	72
65. Movement	73
66. My Son	74
67. Networking	75
68. None of Your Business	76
69. Order	77
70. Passing the Buck	78

71. Ploughing	79
72. Preacher's Kid	80
73. Pushing the Limits	81
74. Routine	82
75. Scaffolding	83
76. Secrets	84
77. Sharing Christmas	85
78. Shortcuts	86
79. Signs	87
80. Sinners Even	88
81. Standing Up	90
82. Stay Out, Cat!	91
83. Stewing	92
84. Such a small Thing	93
85. Tackling Goliath	94
86. Teaching and Learning	95
87. Tell me the Old, Old Story	96
88. To the Congregation	98
89. Today We Remember – Good Friday	99
90. Touched by an Angel	100
91. Umbrellas	101
92. Unwanted Gifts	102
93. Value for Pain	103
94. Visitors	104
95. Waiting on Him	105
96. Weeding	106
97. What a Week	107
98. What's in a Name	109
99. When God says "No"	111
100. Which Destination	112

This book is dedicated to the memory of my mother, Jean Olwyn Morris, who was my greatest teacher, supporter and friend. She went home to be with her Lord and Saviour on 4th September 2014, the day after the last story was written for this book.

x

1

A Start

This particular day started badly. I woke about 5.00 am with thoughts about what I would be able to leave behind if I was to die. I'm renowned for having a very vivid imagination, however, on this particular occasion I was unable to let go of the thoughts that kept going around and around. My brain connected advertisements that I had seen; parts of a sermon on the previous Sunday; some offhand comments from members of my family and some health concerns that were already in my head. The result was that I felt convinced that I was not meant to be here and that my family would be better off if I wasn't either.

I rang my mother as the thoughts threatened to get out of control. I asked her, as I have on many occasions, to "talk some common-sense into me". After that conversation I felt better, realising just how blessed I was that she was there, that I could ring her, knowing that she would pray for me, rather than telling me that I was being really stupid.

Each time I hang up after one of these sessions, I wonder just how many more times I am going to be able to do this. Titus 2:3 says: "The aged women likewise, that they be in behaviour as becometh holiness, not false accusers, not given to much wine, teachers of good things;" In this my mother has been very faithful.

I continually marvel at her faithfulness to God and often have to remember that, while I would love to be able to do what she does, in the way that she does it, I cannot. This is because God has made me a different person with a different personality and a different mission to carry out for Him.

2

A Wheel Bearing

I was driving to town after a bad start one morning, when I heard a new noise in my car, which was ageing fast, and put it down to a couple of tyres in the boot rubbing together. I dropped the tyres off where they were supposed to be, attended Bible Study and then headed to Tenterfield. What I discovered was that the noise was not the tyres rubbing together, as I could still hear it, on and off.

So, I prayed. I pray very often while I'm driving, but this time it was specifically about the noise. I continued to have thoughts about dying, which is why my day had got off to such a bad start. Things like: "I'm glad I'm the only one in the car, that way I won't be killing anyone else if I have an accident" were going through my mind. As the noise continued, I continued to pray: "Lord please keep me safe until I get to Tenterfield and I'll check the car there unless of course, you are planning on calling me home today."

Forty kilometres out of Tenterfield, I suddenly pulled the car over, got out and had a look. In fact, the car looked to be ok. I walked around, no flat tyres, nothing hanging down underneath. For some reason I checked the left wheel bearing and it was ok. I walked around the front of the car, checked the driver's side wheel bearing, and bounced! It was so hot; it burnt my fingers. Ok! I knew then what that squeak was.

Psalm 121:8 says: "The Lord shall preserve thy going out and thy coming in from this time forth, and even for evermore." He had saved me! Death could have been a real possibility if I had carried on.

3

A Blessed Day

My crazy imagination got my day off to an ordinary start but, by the end of the day, I was going to be able to look back and realise just how blessed I was.

During Bible Study, I found out that my son had been left stranded in Casino. Arrangements were made to get him to Tenterfield where I would collect him. A good friend, who had prayed during our prayer time for God's guidance, took my Scripture class. I'm not sure that she expected God to answer her prayer quite so quickly, but I am grateful that she answered the call. And after some other minor juggling, I set off.

My car didn't sound healthy and I eventually pulled over discovering a hot wheel bearing. Had I not stopped when I did, and the wheel bearing had jammed, I would most likely have been on a stretch of road, with a lot of "S" bends and cliff walls on the right, which dropped off into nothing on the left. One way or another, the outcome of a jammed wheel bearing would not have been pretty.

God's care for me was also demonstrated by the arrival of an older NRMA mechanic, who exceeded what he actually had to do and who was willing to go beyond mere duty and kept looking for me outside the designated area

In reading Psalm 37, I find great encouragement as it tells me; not to fret (verse 1), the Lord holds me with his hand (verse 24) and if I trust in Him, he will save me (verse 40).

Will my imagination go crazy again? Of course! But I now have the memories of this day to look back on and see what God did for me and realise that He can do it again as He cares for me.

4

A conversation

I had a conversation with some people, which indicated that they had no idea of the pain that many people were going through as they struggled with a disastrous drought that was happening in our country. Their lack of understanding and the easy solutions that they suggested made me so angry and distressed that I spent many hours in tears. I also prayed for many hours, asking God to forgive me for my anger towards them. I asked Him to help me to deal with my reaction to both situations, their lack of knowledge, and my anger.

Eventually, I realised just how blessed I was to have walked the very tough road that God had led and walked with me through my life. So I thanked God: for having my dreams shattered, for being robbed, for watching my children go without shoes and meat on the table; for being abused; for being misunderstood and judged wrongly; for the nights that I sat up with sick children watching one nearly die; for all the times when I could not see the light at the end of the tunnel and other struggles that I have pushed into the back of my mind. Oh, what a blessing it is to know and understand the desire to not want to get up and keep going; to want to throw in the towel and call it quits, because this means that my heart feels for those people who have to walk in that valley.

Finally, I could see that Romans 8:28 "And we know that all things work together for good to them that love God, to them who are the called according to His purpose" was right, even if that purpose was to be able to relate in some small way to those people who struggle.

5

A Day to Forget

I have been praying a lot this week about what to post for Mother's Day. This morning, I thought about how I have already celebrated Mother's Day this week. I had the pleasure of a cuppa with two daughters; I spoke with my mother over the phone on Thursday and again this morning, and I anticipate a visit from my sons today. So many blessings! Yet, God made me think about all those mothers who don't have these blessings. What about the women who have no children, the mothers who are facing their first Mother's Day without a child? Think about the mothers whose children have abused them, forgotten them, or just don't care? How about you give them a special thought. SO:

Dear Lord,
You know all those women who would rather forget what this day is supposed to celebrate, who are sad, lonely, and hurting badly. I ask that you wrap your arms around every one of them, give them comfort and help them to see one little thing to make them smile. Amen.

I continued to think about the women in the Bible who also had to deal with the disappointment of being "barren". There would have been a great many others who were scorned all their lives because they did not produce offspring.

God did, however, have good reasons for answering the prayers of Sarah and Hannah in particular. These answers also had their challenges to be met; Sarah had to watch Ishmael be nasty to Isaac (Genesis 21:8-12) and Hannah had to leave her child in God's temple. He was just getting to that very cute stage, a stage that most mothers really enjoy. (1 Samuel 1:24). Whatever God's plan is, it will be the best, but not easy, regardless of its design.

6

A Few More Steps

Feeding the dogs one afternoon, I discovered that the storage box didn't contain enough dog food to go around our pack. There was no assistance to be had from other members of the family since they were all away working, so I had to replenish the supplies by myself. While the new bags weren't miles away, I still had to carry the twenty-two kilos some distance. Now, this is not something I do every day and I was finding the bag heavy and slippery. As I closed the distance between me and the empty container, I was losing my grip.

With each step I prayed, "Lord please help with these last few steps." I was thinking that often I have asked God to do things for me instead of giving me the strength, imagination, and determination to finish a job or to get through a difficult time.

God doesn't promise to make our lives easy. In fact, the Bible tells us that as Christians our lives are going to be very difficult. Mathew 5:11 says "Blessed are ye, when men shall revile you and persecute you and shall say all manner of evil against you falsely, for my sake."

I remember the first time that I realised that Paul got exhausted during his missionary journeys (2 Corinthians 1:8) and yet he was still able to say: "I can do all things through Christ which strengtheneth me" (Philippians 4:13).

Extending the muscles in my body strengthens them and yes, I know that I will be in pain for a day or two, but eventually, they will be stronger. The same goes for my spiritual muscles, the more they are used, the stronger they will get. Thank you, God, for the daily spiritual workouts.

7

A Good Mechanic

I was sitting on the side of the road with a wheel bearing that wasn't going to get me to the next town. I needed to do something other than drive on. A couple of phone calls and the NRMA would be out in about an hour.

All the thoughts I had entertained earlier in the day about dying were gone. I was left with a feeling of complete calm and security. I read my book while I waited for the truck to arrive. I occasionally asked God if He could make it sooner but felt completely safe as truck after truck rattled past me and yes, I felt the car move as every one of them passed.

Finally, the NRMA truck drove past and eventually came back. It turned out that he had been looking for a red car, even though I had informed the operator that my car was light green. I was also told that I was actually outside their district. This meant that had I got a younger driver; I would have been waiting much longer, as they do not go past the regional borders. The driver stopped to allow me to collect my son, (which was the reason that I was driving to Tenterfield in the first place) as we drove past the service station, where he was still waiting for me to arrive. What amazed the mechanic was that the steering was not behaving as would be expected, explaining why I did not realise what was wrong. When the mechanic checked the bearing, it fell apart. The bearing could have come apart while I was driving, and the result would have been disastrous. The car was repaired and we drove home, arriving safely about seven that night. Psalm 121:8 "The Lord shall preserve thy going out and thy coming in from this time forth, and even forevermore."

On this day He certainly did!

8

A Light at the end of a Tunnel

How many times do we say this when life has been uncertain for a while and we think that uncertainty is coming to an end? I know have remarked in this manner many times. I've even had friends suggest that the light I can see at the end of the said tunnel is a train coming to flatten me once more.

We all experience periods in life when there just doesn't seem to be any end to the number of trials and tribulations that we face on a daily basis, with many of them overlapping each other. For instance, a child may be chronically ill but there is work to be carried out and if there are other children in the family, their needs also need to be seen to. Often accidents happen during these periods because sleep deprivation takes its toll on our ability to concentrate. You find yourself asking 'What else can go wrong?'

I'm at that age when getting up during the night is pretty much a given activity. Each time I do I make sure that I switch on my bedside lamp simply because as I return to my room, I need a light to guide me! I have lost count of the number of times that I have stumbled in the hallway simply because of the lack of a light. It doesn't matter how bright or small the light is, it just helps me to find my way back to bed.

When we are struggling to get through those very stressful times in our lives let us remember the words of Jesus "Then spake Jesus again unto them, saying, I am the light of the world: he that followeth me shall not walk in darkness, but shall have the light of life." John 8:12. He is our light because we can trust Him to care for us no matter what.

9

A Torch Beam

The morning had been one of those that made you feel like you should go back to bed and start again! As the morning progressed there just seemed to be more and more issues to be dealt with. Yet that wasn't possible. I had to keep going. I was in a very dark place. So distressed and overwhelmed by all the issues, I cried out for something positive to help me carry on. I felt I really needed a torchlight to help me to keep going. I shared my problems with a Christian work colleague. We prayed for God to give me some affirmative encouragement, we even went as far as making some suggestions about what might help.

About lunchtime, I received a phone call which told me that one of the issues had been dealt with by someone else in a very practical manner and in a much better way than I would have handled it. There was my positive encouragement! God had answered my prayers, but He had not used any one of the suggestions that I had given Him. Should this have surprised me? Absolutely not!

I'm reminded of Isaiah 55:8-9 "For my thoughts are **not** your thoughts, neither are your ways my ways, says the Lord. For as the Heavens are higher than the earth, so are my ways higher than your ways, and my thoughts than your thoughts."

Psalm 26:14 says, "Wait on the Lord: be of good courage, and he shall strengthen thine heart: wait I say, on the Lord."

Even in the little things such as encouragement, God has a very different answer to what we might expect. There will always be times when I will be overwhelmed, but God has a torch beam every time.

10

A Wonderful Teacher

I often think about and remember a wonderful old lady who used to be a member of our church. I remember her tenacity. At her funeral, I had the privilege to speak of her generosity, honesty, and frankness that we would all do well to imitate. In our Women's Bible Study group, you knew what she believed and want she wanted. Her generosity was something that will not be forgotten soon. We have missed her love of life. Her determination is something that I personally would like to be able to replicate in my life.

I have a Cassia Tree that this lady gave me to replace one that had snapped off and I had intended to plant it in the same place where the other tree had been. I had set it down beside the carport. It had put down roots through the bottom of the pot. There was no way it was going to be moved. As I drove home one day, thinking about this I realised that this lady was a bit like that tree, she did not allow small difficulties to get in her way. There were many times when she refused to allow me to make her a cup of tea because if she didn't keep doing it herself, she would lose the ability to do things all together.

How many times do I stop doing things just because it's getting too hard? In 2 Corinthians 1:8, Paul tells of how he despaired about how tired he was at times and how he had to trust in God to carry on. I know that this wonderful lady would have been able to relate to Paul many times in her life, but she did carry on until the end. Will we follow her example and the example of others who have been so faithful to their Father in Heaven?

11

Battle Weary

During a discussion about a particular problem, the comment was made; "I think people are too tired to fight anymore." There have been many times when I have said much the same thing concerning my problems, particularly if they have taken a very long time to be solved.

This time, however, I thought about things a little differently. What was a long time for God? How many years did the people of Israel have to wait for God to let them into the Promised Land? How many days did Jesus stay in the Wilderness? What would happen if God ran out of patience waiting for us to answer His call? 2 Peter 3:8, tells us "But do not forget this one thing, dear friends: With the Lord, a day is like a thousand years, and a thousand years are like a day." And verse nine says: "The Lord is not slow in keeping his promise, as some understand slowness. He is patient with you, not wanting anyone to perish, but everyone to come to repentance."

The people of Israel wandered in the wilderness for forty years, and Jesus fasted for forty days. We are so used to things being "instant" that I feel we sometimes expect God to change His ways to the "instant variety" as well. God does not change; "Jesus Christ, the same yesterday, and today and forever." (Hebrews 13:8).

Life will always be a battle. It is that way because sin has entered the world. God wants us to carry on with faith in His strength, so that when we reach the end, He will be able to take great delight in saying, "Come, you who are blessed by my Father; take your inheritance, the kingdom prepared for you since the creation of the world." (Matthew 25:34).

12

Being Winners

One day I was playing my favourite game of "Spider". I was halfway through a game, thinking I should be able to win this one. However, experience has taught me that often when you start to feel comfortable, all of a sudden, life throws a spanner in the works and life gets tough.

Understanding why things have got tough is probably the toughest thing to do. We will ask questions like: What have I done wrong? Job's friends told him that he must have done something wrong. (Job 4:7-9). Did I take my eyes off God? Peter took his eyes off Jesus while walking on the water and the certainty literally fell out from under his feet! (Matthew 14: 22-33). Who's to blame for this? The disciples asked Jesus whose sin it was that caused the blindness of the man who was told to go and wash in the Pool of Siloam. (John 9:1-6).

Every difficulty that comes our way, while not sent by God, will be used by God. It will help to strengthen us, teach us, and help us reach others. 2 Thessalonians 2:15-17 reads, "So then, brothers, stand firm and hold to the teachings we passed on to you, whether by word of mouth or by letter. May our Lord Jesus Christ himself and God our Father, who loved us and by His grace gave us eternal encouragement and good hope, encourage your hearts and strengthen you in every good deed and word."

While it is hard to feel like a winner in the midst of trouble, we do need to remind ourselves that if we stay faithful, one day we will be winners, in the eyes of God, on Judgement Day.

13

Caring

This word and what it means is something that I have been thinking about a lot. It started out because I was encouraged by someone who cared! That encouragement meant so much to me because I had had a bad day in the previous week, leaving me questioning my self-worth. I got annoyed with myself. Recently I have been struggling with matters like this a lot. I remembered that I had also struggled with bigger issues a few years ago, but I had had a wonderful couple to support me. God has moved them on now, probably to give them a break from my constant need for care! I thought about how some people seem to think that the more fuss you make about issues the more you care! I understand why people believe actions speak louder than words. Making a fuss, however, to me just screams "I care about me looking good more than I care about your need".

Jesus had plenty to say about the Pharisees and their need to look good to the people of Israel while he was on earth. See Matthew 15:1-9.

Real care can be shown just by sitting quietly with someone, doing the washing up without being asked or quietly slipping someone some money. There is no requirement for anyone else to even know that you have done these things. Jesus even recommends in Matthew 6:1 "Be careful that you don't do your charitable giving before men, to be seen by them, or else you have no reward from your Father who is in heaven Be careful that you don't do your charitable giving before men, to be seen by them, or else you have no reward from your Father who is in heaven." (WEB) The most important person in the world will always see what you do and why you do it. The Bible tells us that He will call us all to account on the Day of Judgement in Matthew 25:31-46.

14

Christmas Night

Just before Christmas one year, I was collecting my son from work at around midnight each night. I got into the habit of looking at the sky as I got into the car. One particular night, I remember, it was perfectly black velvet with silver stars all over it. It was so clear and calm; I thought, "A perfect Luke 2:1-20". Later I began to wonder why I would have considered that sort of sky to be a Christmas night sky. The Bible says in Luke: 2-8, "And there were in the same country shepherds abiding in the field, keeping watch over their flock by night". It doesn't tell us what sort of night it was. Yet hymns and stories have been written that give the impression of a clear, calm, silent night sky.

Is it something to do with the fact that on such nights we would not expect anything dramatic to happen? If the night had been stormy with flashes of lightning all around them, maybe the shepherds wouldn't have been surprised if an angel of Lord had appeared to them. Isn't it in those quiet, silent days or nights when life seems to be good that we least expect disaster, drama, or death?

Yet God will call as many of us home on these types of days as He does on stormy, bad days. He will cut into our history when He wants to, not when we are ready.

We all need to be prepared for when God says: "It's time, right now! Come and give an account of your life". Death, disaster, or trouble will never come when it is convenient for us, but in God's time, which will be better for us even if we don't understand it then.

15

Clang, Clang, Clang!

I was thinking about the changes in our business world. It seems to be taken as absolutely right that "Bigger is better". I suspect that the church has taken on board this thinking as well, even if they don't realize it.

I watched a television program about an immigrant, who bought land and became a successful farmer. He is still successful; he has educated his kids. One of them is now planning on taking over the business. The business is still on the original acreage. He never gave in to the temptation of expanding. Yet he is still hailed as being a great example of success.

1 Corinthians 13:1 says, "Though I speak with the tongues of men and of angels, and have not charity, I am become *as* sounding brass, or a tinkling cymbal." Verse 13 says "And now abideth faith, hope, charity, these three; but the greatest of these *is* charity."

The problem as I see it is that love for the wrong thing is going to create more strife. Big businesses are only showing love for big profits and not for the person who would like to run a corner store. The small business, whatever it is, is insignificant, and should be disposed of.

The successful churches and Christians are the ones that get on with the plan that God has for them and are faithful to Him. For those that are in small churches, remember, bigger churches are in danger of not seeing to the needs of every member and missing even one person's personal need can be considered a failure.

If we want God to say to us on judgment day "Well done, good and faithful servant" (Matthew 25:23) then being faithful is what is required.

16

Clear Vision

I started out for town one morning, but it wasn't until I rounded a corner and found myself driving into the sun that I discovered how dirty and dusty my windscreen was. A flick of the windscreen lever, water squirting up and the movement of the wipers fixed the problem quickly.

It brought to mind how the average person, living a life that they have chosen, can be travelling along very nicely "thank you" and then suddenly they round a corner in that life and find that things really are not as clear as they thought. If we are willing to listen, God will show us just who He is and how much He loves us and that He is the way to Salvation.

I'm also reminded that, for Christians, sometimes we can think that we are seeing some spiritual truth clearly, then something happens and we get a completely different perspective on what we think. "But the wisdom that is from above is first pure, then peaceable, gentle, *and* easy to be intreated, full of mercy and good fruits, without partiality, and without hypocrisy." James 3:17.

It doesn't matter how many times we read our Bible or how long we live. God will always be able to teach us something new each day, as we allow the Holy Spirit to work in us. Keep looking for God's lessons each day and He will surprise you.

17

Coming Home

We had been away and as we travelled, I looked at the gardens that we passed. As we arrived home, I looked at my garden which was filled with winter flowers and exclaimed, "And suddenly my garden looks very pretty!" What had the gardens been like, that I had been looking at while we had been travelling? There were tidy lawns and flowering shrubs but as I look back, I don't remember seeing lots of flower beds or lots of colour.

Turning these images over in my head, it has made me wonder if that is what it's going to be like when we get to Heaven. Will it be like coming home and seeing the real beauty that God has in store for us?

When we read Revelation, we get an idea of how beautiful the heavenly Jerusalem will be: "Having the glory of God; and her light was like unto a stone most precious, even like a jasper stone, clear as crystal." (Revelation 21:11).

Now I'm not being conceited, there is no way my garden is anywhere near as pretty as what will be in heaven, of that I am sure. My garden has lots of weeds in it to start with and there will be none of those in heaven. What I think God is trying to show me is that it's about the contrast between earth and Heaven. While being away was nice and the gardens were clean and tidy, they weren't pretty.

Here on earth we make the best of what life gives us. This is a bit like those clean tidy gardens with the splashes of colour but are mostly dull and uninteresting. In contrast, Heaven will be pretty, beautiful, spectacular, and filled with colour. Now that is one of the things to look forward to!

I was awake thinking about the tragedies that we are hearing about nearly all the time lately. It even occurred to me that it might be time for Jesus to return. Then of course I remembered that when I was younger, I wanted to do things before Jesus returned and I know that there are many young people out there who would feel the same. In fact, I have a couple of projects of my own that I would still like to see finished. The next thought was, "I could die tomorrow, and the projects wouldn't be finished anyway."

We fear what we don't know and in the back of my mind, I suspect that if Jesus was to return right now, we wouldn't miss out on anything except pain. Will young women have children to look after? I'm pretty sure they will. Will husbands and wives still be able to have a relationship? I'm pretty sure they will - they just won't have the issues that trip us up here on earth. All our relationships will be perfect in that we will understand each other's needs and thinking patterns- and you know what? I can't wait!

In Revelation 22:1-3a we read, "And He shewed me a pure river of water of life, clear as crystal, proceeding out of the throne of God and of the Lamb. In the midst of the street of it and on either side of the river, was there the tree of life, which bare twelve manner of fruits, and yielded her fruit every month; and the leaves of the tree were for the healing of the nations. And there shall be no more curse."

18

Crying Out

As a sheep farmer's wife, there are particular nights of the year that I do not look forward to. Those nights are the ones when the lambs have been taken from their mothers. As a result, they spend a large part of the night bleating. The noise carries across the paddocks, regardless of how far they are away from the house. Now, being separated from their mothers is a necessary part of their lives. It enables the lambs to grow stronger and faster and gives the ewes recovery time. It is, however, an unpleasant time for them and us.

Thinking about these events one night, I realised that there are many people in the world who are also crying out. Unlike the lambs that know what is wrong, many people would not even know what the problem is or who is able to solve it.

In Isaiah 40:3 we are told that John the Baptist would be 'a voice crying in the wilderness'. He also knew what was wrong. People were sinners. He was preparing the way for Jesus; Letting people know that Jesus was the answer to their problems. Jesus was the way to salvation. Jesus was the way to Heaven. "I am the way and the truth and the life. No-one comes to the Father except through me." (John 14:6).

There are times when we will cry to God, not really knowing what we need. When we listen to His voice, He is faithful and tells us what we need and give us the solution, there are many people that we know who are crying and don't know what is missing in their lives. It is up to us to pray for them and tell them the good news. Jesus is the answer.

19

Damaged

In the garden, there was a tree that needed to be dealt with. It had been damaged not only by a vine growing up through the branches but also from winds during a storm. The branches had been weighed down under the extra burden but when the storm winds blew they snapped. As I pulled out the vine and dragged it and the broken limbs to the rubbish heap, I was thinking about all those people who could relate to this tree.

They carry so much extra stress or workloads and seem to manage to cope until, out of the blue a storm hits. It could be an illness, job loss or the death of a loved one. Something has to give, and it usually does. If they are left to fend for themselves their lives continue but like that tree, parts of their lives are left hanging and dying and they take on an ugly look.

My tree didn't get a choice; I forced my care for it on it without asking permission. For us humans though when we are broken or damaged, we know that God loves us. When we allow Him to care for us and all we have to do is ask Him, He will give us the strength to move forward despite the damage and things that are now missing in our lives. He will help us to grow stronger, develop new interests and bring out in us those talents that He knows are there but maybe have been hidden for too long.

For proof let us check what the Bible tells us "Cast thy burden upon the LORD, and he shall sustain thee: he shall never suffer the righteous to be moved." Psalm 55:22 "Casting all your care upon him; for He careth for you." 1 Peter 5:7.

20

Death, Jail, or Jesus

We were discussing with a fellow Christian the behaviour of some people who were not doing what they should have done. They made a statement: there are three outcomes, death, jail, or Jesus Christ. Turning this over later it struck me as more profound than I first thought. Yes, the wages of sin is death, the consequences here on earth can be jail but the way out is Jesus Christ.

First: death: the wages of sin is death "For the wages of sin is death; but the gift of God is eternal life through Jesus Christ our Lord" (Romans 6:23). This may mean that people do something so wrong that it does result in the physical death of themselves or sadly the death of an innocent bystander. Ultimately though, if we continue to leave Jesus out of our lives, then when we physically die, we will come face to face with God without our Saviour to intercede for us and we then face the eternal death in hell.

Second: Jail: When people break the laws that are set down to ensure the safety of society then the consequences will be a jail sentence. Now many will say that only happens if you get caught. The Bible tells us that we are slaves to sin, so even if it isn't a human jail there is a spiritual, mental, and emotional jail that we get locked into. "His own iniquities shall take the wicked himself, and he shall be caught with the cords of his sins." (Proverbs 5:22).

Third: the way out is Jesus Christ: Jesus tells us Himself that the only way we can have eternal life is through Him "...I am the way, the truth, and the life: no man cometh unto the Father, but by me." (John 14:6). This is why He died on the cross. Have you asked Him to save you?

21

Depression and Bullies; Part 1

We talk a lot about how bad it is for children to be bullied. We cry in horror when teenagers take their lives because of it. Yet, as we grow into adults, we realise that it doesn't stop there. As I look back on the times, I have struggled the most, I realise that there were many bullies in my life.

They weren't my bosses or my neighbours (even though I had some of them). They were those in society who decided that they knew better than anyone else what was right or wrong. They attacked my thinking when I read books written by these people. The constant barrage over the media criticizing not only how I but other parents as well, raised our kids, was at times overwhelming.

Now that my children have flown the nest, I still find there are still plenty of bullies in our lives. These people are usually extreme animal activists or big supermarket chain stores telling us how to or not to do our job as farmers or what price they will pay.

We even find that there are members within the church who still think that unless we are living our lives in the same manner as they are, we are not doing things correctly.

It also seems to me that the more blessings a person has, the greater the bully. It is very easy to think that what works for us will work for everyone else. Sometimes that will be the case but not always. So, before we try to tell the rest of the world about the love of God, let us make sure that we are doing what the Bible tells us in James 3:13: "Who is a wise man and endued with knowledge among you? Let him shew out of a good conversation his works with meekness of wisdom." Let us tell the message of love, lovingly to all those around us.

22

Depression and Bullies; Part 2

Bullies contribute to the battle with depression. It should be easy to not listen to these nasty voices and many people would tell us that we shouldn't listen to them. As a society, it seems to me that we like watching people being bullied. This I think is reflected in the popularity ratings of so-called "Reality Shows". When we watch these shows, what we see on the screen is bad enough, what they edited out I can only imagine. After listening to a report by a woman who had been a contestant, I'm pretty certain that very little of it is good.

Why do people bully others? I think there is more to it than just trying to make themselves feel better. It is much easier to operate things if everyone is doing the same thing and in the same way. This is not a thing we as humans do naturally, so bullying becomes a means of herding people into the same way of thinking. We have seen many countries try this in the past.

I started to think about how much the Jews were bullied during the time of Jesus. After all they had the Romans (the biggest bullies in history) on one hand, telling them what they could and could not do. Then on the other hand they had the Pharisees telling them how they should be living their lives, even though those Pharisees didn't even follow their own rules.

Psalm 139: 14a says, "I will praise thee; for I am fearfully and wonderfully made; marvellous are thy works...." We are all individuals whom God loves individually.

This in turn made me think about the courage of the disciples of Jesus. Their courage was evident in the way they followed Jesus around the country. Peter and John were fishermen, how much strength and courage did it take for them to go out each night and fish on the Sea of Galilee. This is a sea, with a surface that can be as still as glass one moment and toss a boat around and swallow it up the next.

Matthew came to mind as well. Here was a man who dared to take on a job as a Tax Collector for the Romans. It was a job that was despised by the Jews. Did he take the job on as a means of funding some sort of charity work? Was he an honest man? He could have been! We assume he wasn't because, at the time, people who worked in this industry had the reputation for being very dishonest. He was obviously educated otherwise he wouldn't have been able to write the book of Matthew. Did his job fund some sort of underground political movement against the Romans?

It is only speculation on my part, but what courage did he display? Even without this guesswork, his courage was evident when he resigned his position upon being called by Jesus to be a disciple. The Romans could have had him killed or thrown into prison. It was a time when courage was needed both before and after the death of Christ and His ascension.

God instructed Joshua to, "Only be thou strong and very courageous, ...". Joshua 1:7.

God wants us all to find that courage as well, the courage that He will give us if we follow Him. It's a courage that will get us through each day regardless of what it holds.

23

Different Angle

There are two ways, it seems, to look at the same object. I remember a paddock of wheat my father grew when we were teenagers. My brothers took two photos of this crop. If you look at one photo you are led to believe that it is full of thistles. Look at the other photo, taken on the same day; it looks like a very clean crop with very few weeds.

This is just like the two versions of an Early Morning Prayer. The English Version says: 'Lord, grant that I may not be like porridge, Stiff, Stodgy and Hard to Stir. But like cornflakes, Crisp, Fresh and Ready to Serve'. On the other hand, the Scottish Version says: Lord, grant that I may not be like cornflakes, Light-weight, Brittle and Cold. But like porridge, Warm, Comforting and Full of Goodness'.

We are told that a glass can be either half full or half empty. So how would God want me to see things? For many years, I wandered in the wilderness, of stress, trials, and pain. It is only with age and maturity that I have been able to see that God has really blessed my life so abundantly. So many blessings I was unable to see with the eyes of youth.

As I look back, He has taught me so much. Yes, I would have loved to have learnt these lessons any other way, but God decided to teach me His way and I have enough maturity now to realize that His ways are better than mine.

"So is my word that goes out from my mouth: It will not return to me empty, but will accomplish what I desire and achieve the purpose for which I sent it." Isaiah 55:11.

So, the challenge is to change the angle of view.

24

Don't judge a book by its cover

We all look at the cover of a book and try to make a judgement about whether we would like to read it or not. If the cover is bright and cheerful, we are more likely to have a more positive response to it than if the cover is dull and boring. What is our response if the cover is torn and tattered, I wonder?

Many people, non-Christians particularly, judge our God by what they see in the people that serve Him. As a child I heard that the only Bible some people read is the people they see. When they see Christians not fulfilling a contract, taking fruit off a tree without asking, even when it might be hanging over a fence, telling lies or being rude, they think they are seeing the work of God.

Please don't judge my God on my behaviour, I am not perfect, I am a sinner, saved by God. I am, however, still human and I make mistakes. I am not a Bible. I am only the cover - a battered, torn and damaged cover at that.

If you want to really see my God, you need to open His Word. Read the real message for yourself. Ask Him to help you understand the message of just how much He loves you. How He sent Jesus to die on the cross so that you too can be saved! How, once you have gone to Him and asked Him into your life, you will inherit eternal life.

Please find a Bible and open it at St John and start reading there and then decide how good God is.

If you find what He says is true, then go to Him with this prayer:

"Father, I know that you love me, I know that I have been wrong, please forgive me and show me what you want me to do. Amen"

25

Dreams and Plans

The conversation was all about our hopes and dreams and how hard it was to make them happen. How others appeared to have given up and support was unforthcoming. Reflecting on this conversation later forced me to think about my own dreams and what I knew about others who had worked very hard to make their dreams a reality.

Dreams and plans are very good; we all need them. They give us something to look forward to. Dreams, however, should most importantly be part of God's plan for our lives. "Are my dreams part of your plan for me Lord?" is my constant prayer. Any dream that is not part of God's plan for our lives will always be harder to make happen than the one that is centred on doing the will of God.

When someone appears to have given up on their dreams, it is most likely a case of "appearances can be deceiving". Sometimes our bigger dreams need to be put on hold in order to allow us to eat, have a bed to sleep in and a roof over our heads, along with many other things that are necessary for us to live long enough to make the dreams come true.

What of my own dreams! Yes, they had been put on hold in order to allow me to raise my children, all five of them to the best of my ability. Also putting my dreams aside for a while allowed my husband to achieve his dream! That doesn't mean that my dream has been abandoned all together. I used what little spare time I had available to learn a variety of skills and in fact some of the learning did not seem to be related to my dreams at all. It is only in hindsight that I can see that the pieces of the puzzles fit together in some sort of a funny fashion. God has led me in a variety of directions which has given me a much richer experience of life and that has enhanced my existence beyond any dream that I might have had. Modern technology has also been invented and is constantly changing, which is making my dreams much easier to realize than they once would have been.

While I understand that it is very hard to see a dream in a long-term view for young people, God has a couple of things that we need to keep in mind. In Ecclesiastes 3:1 He says, "To everything there is a season, and a time to every purpose under the heaven." The other thing that we need to remember is what He tells us in Isaiah 55:8 "For my thoughts are not your thoughts, neither are your ways my ways, saith the Lord."

I still have some dreams that I would like to see fulfilled. In fact, I thought one would be fulfilled this year, but that is not to be. I have often discussed this dream with others and my final analysis about it is this: It is not the "be all and end all" of my life because the "be all and end all" of my life is to go to heaven to be with my Heavenly Father and family. This is the ultimate 'dream' and I would much rather have that one come true than anything I could image while I am here on earth.

26

Easter Sunday – We Celebrate

It was suggested to me once, that I might feel guilty if I did not visit my parents more often. Living so far away and being farmers, getting time to visit my parents had not been easy over the years and – 'Yes!', visits had been few and far between. I had never felt guilty, so I asked them "why?"

"How would you feel if you get a phone call tomorrow to say they had died?" was their reply.

Thinking about this question, my response was that I knew where they were going, and while it might take me twenty years, I would find them waiting for me in Heaven. Of course, once the question had been asked, I had to make it a point of discussion during my weekly phone call with my mother. "Why would you feel guilty, if we die before you come to see us again, we will be waiting in Heaven for you," was Mum's comeback. Of course, this confidence could only exist because of Easter Sunday.

HE IS RISEN! Yes! He is risen! We celebrate that death did not hold Jesus in the grave, that He defeated death. If we accept that Jesus died and rose again for us, if we come to Jesus, thanking Him for what He did and ask Him to wash away our sins. He can present us to His Father, as righteous people on Judgement Day.

John 14:2 tells us, "In my father's house are many mansions; if it were not so I would have told you. I go to prepare a place for you. And if I go and prepare a place for you, I will come again, and receive you unto myself; that where I am, there you may be also."

This Sunday if you are saved through Jesus you can celebrate with confidence.

27

Eating Right

A church we attended had stopped preaching the true word of God. We decided not to move because we felt that God wanted us to stay and pray about the issues, helping those who also felt the same way. We eventually found out there were many others with the same concerns; it was just that no one was saying so out loud. Confronting the church leaders about our concerns seemed to be a pointless exercise. Matthew 7:6b says "... neither cast ye your pearls before swine, lest they trample them under their feet, and turn again and rend you." So, we stayed and prayed.

Many of our friends, however, were concerned that we would be starved spiritually if we stayed and yes, that was worrying me as well. Driving home one day, turning this over in my head, I realised that it was up to me to feed myself in the midst of this. As a child, I had a lot of allergies and my parents were very careful not to have any food in the house that could make me sick. As an adult, my allergy list grew even longer. I found that I had to make sure that I had sufficient food in the house that I could eat so I could disregard the foods that would make me sick even though they were being eaten by other members of the family.

If I can do this on a physical level, then I can do it on a spiritual level. In Acts 2:42 we read "and they continued steadfastly in the apostles' doctrine and fellowship and in breaking of bread and in prayers." These people met, not as we know today as the established church so if I surround myself with true believers and enjoy their fellowship, even though it is not an established environment, then I will continue to eat well.

28

Equality of Men and Women

One reader wrote to me after reading my story "International Day for Women" was posted on my website, with the following:

"Your thoughts on women were insightful. We tend to read comments negatively as though it was our fault, and we thus have a lower view of ourselves. I wonder if part of the problem (and I notice you didn't touch on it in the blog) is the effect of radical feminism on society and on men in particular where men no longer know what their role is."

I searched and found the following **Definition:** Radical feminism is a philosophy emphasizing the patriarchal roots of inequality between men and women, or, more specifically, social dominance of women by men.

As I prayed about this, I realised that while my message was directed at women, it is still applicable to both men and women. Yes, we do tend to receive messages in a negative tone, most likely because of the effect of "original sin". This is the way the devil likes it, if we get the message wrong in the first instance then the multiplication of negative messages can compound sin as they pile up on top of each other. After all, the first negative message was heard by Eve, from the serpent, in the Garden of Eden.

Why do men apparently no longer know what their role is in our current society? It is because they are also listening to the world instead of the Word of God. God tells men that they are also made in His image but that He has given them a woman to be a helpmate and that makes her his equal even though he has a position as head of the household. Maybe society has in the past told men that the only way to be the head is to be a dominant figurehead and maybe put women down to keep them in their place.

If we listen to God's word, He will tell us that we are to love each other and the husband must love his wife in the same manner that God loves the Church. (Ephesians 5:25). So, if men listen to God instead of Society, then they will be able to still be head of the family even when the wife has to be the major income provider, because it's about knowing that she is there helping him provide for the family, regardless of how that is done.

The most common story that I have heard about the problem that men have is "do they open the door for a woman or let her open it herself". If a woman is rude to a man because he has opened the door for her, he can look to Christ and be polite back because that is what Christ would have done. He doesn't have to listen to the negative message which is "I'm better than you" or "You are putting me down by treating me politely". As hard as it is, all he has to hear, all he has to understand, is that she is rude and that he has behaved politely instead. It still comes down to showing respect for all those around us, both men and women, and the Christian community is supposed to be the leader in this change of attitude, without being legalistic about it. We do this not because it is the way it should be, but because Christ showed us how to do this while He walked upon the earth.

29

Far from Home

We woke one morning to find that we had a strange dog visiting our home. It was lost. It was obvious that it was loved because it was well fed, if not a little too well, it was wearing a jacket to keep it warm, and a clean shining coat told of loving care. There were however some scars from some sort of fight in his distant past.

We made many phone calls to several neighbours with no success. Our next strategy was to place a photo on Facebook in the hope that many of my friends would share the photo and the owner would contact us.

Later that night my son received a call from the owner. It turned out that the dog had been recently staying with the owner's brother and it seems that it wanted to return there. It had got lost on its way back and had travelled many miles before stopping at our place.

As I thought about the dog and its journey, I realised that it was a lot like many humans. We are all loved by our God. He looks after us and He cares for us even if we don't acknowledge that care or love. Like the dog we run off, chasing other loves and desires and we get lost and hurt.

How do we find our way home? Unlike the dog, our owner (God) knows exactly where we are and He will reach out and rescue us.

Psalm 139:2-4 tells us "Thou knowest my downsitting and mine uprising, thou understandest my thought afar off. Thou compassest my path and my lying down, and are acquainted with all my ways. For there is not a word in my tongue, but, lo, oh Lord, thou knowest it altogether."

We are never far from our loving Father.

30

Farmer's Friends

You have to admire God's sense of humour sometimes. I was out in the garden again, cutting down a weed called 'farmer's friend' and wondering why such a name would be given to such a pest of a plant. It is a plant that has a million seeds that stick to you and getting rid of them is hard work. When you start removing them you find them in all sorts of places, and you are left wondering how on earth they found their way into such spaces. I ended up covered in them from my hair to the cuffs of my jeans. The best part of dealing with these things is when you put the seeds in the fire to dispose of them and hear them pop just like popcorn.

As I debated all the issues attached to the name and properties of this weed, I kept thinking about another friend, Jesus. It was then that I realized that Jesus and this weed had a few things in common.

Firstly, it does not matter how far we get away from Jesus, He will always find us. He sticks to us just like the seeds of that weed.

Secondly, just like those seeds that prickle us, so when we have sins that need to be dealt with, Jesus will prick our consciences constantly until you let Him deal with them. Just like those seeds being popped in the fire so our sins are got rid of. Yes, it may take a while to remove all the seeds and come out clean, but Jesus will be there the whole time helping us to find every last one of them.

"In whom we have redemption through His blood, the forgiveness of sins, according to the riches of His grace;..." (Ephesians 1:7).

31

Feeling Important

I've read articles that try to explain the behaviour of mass shooters as being a way to fulfil their need to be recognised and to have their taste of fame, even if they are not alive to see it happen. We live in an environment that causes many people to recede into their homes away from the outside world more and more. The outcome of this is that many people feel as if they are invisible.

I realised that, like many people, I want to feel important. I find myself being conned by the worldly thinking that tells us that, unless we are known by most of the world, we are not important. Each time I check my website, my book's Facebook page or I still see my unsold books, I find myself saying "What is the point? I am not meant to do this - Why bother?"

I didn't write my first book to be a best seller, and yet I find myself being disappointed that it's not. On the occasions when I offer to speak and I'm turned down, I despair of ever being recognised for what I know I can do to help others.

What I need to remember is that God didn't ask me to write a best seller. He asked me to write the articles so that the few people who read them would be encouraged and find the strength to get up again after they have fallen down. It was also important that I tell the truth and show people that God has a plan for their salvation and a plan for their lives.

We are all important because He made us in His image. "And God said, Let, us make man in our image, after our likeness:" Genesis 1:26a

32

Focus

God had given me a couple of projects to do while I was waiting for the next step in my life. After about two weeks, I found myself feeling a little bit discouraged. It wasn't that things weren't getting done. I wasn't even sure what it was that was making me feel despondent. During a phone call from a friend telling me of all their troubles, they made a remark about how they felt "broken". I reassured them that they weren't – they were only bent and a little bit cracked and that they would get through this period of trouble. It would not last forever.

The early hours of the next morning found me praying for them and thinking about the things that I should have said instead. Things like: "Strap yourself to the Cross when the wind blows too hard and stay safe there", or "Wrap your arms around Jesus and remember that He is carrying you".

Suddenly, I realized that I needed to take my own advice. I had shifted my focus from Jesus to my projects. There was nothing wrong with the projects; I was just focused on the wrong thing. Here was the reason for the loss of motivation, the tiredness that just seemed to creep in. Once the focus was shifted back to where it should be, I started to feel better.

Psalm 121 came to mind, and as I was reading, Psalm 123:1-2 caught my attention. "I lift my eyes to you, to you whose throne is in heaven. As the eyes of slaves look to the hand of their master, as the eyes of a maid look to the hand of her mistress, so our eyes look to the Lord our God, till he shows us His mercy."

Where is your focus?

33

Fog

I woke one winter's morning just as the dawn was breaking. Looking out my bedroom window towards the mountains, I could see a clear, cloudless sky, which promised a warm day. As I watched the sky brighten I noticed a patchy fog roll in over the valley. I thought about those people living in those parts of the valley and how their perspective of the day would be so different. They were waking up to a morning surrounded by gloomy mist that would hinder their vision on where they were going. Would they be able to see 10 feet, 20 feet in front of them? That would depend on how thick the fog was at their place.

This got me thinking about the times in our lives when we are unable to see clearly where our lives are going. We have to move forward, but we have not got a clear idea of where we are meant to go. We can only move slowly, holding the hand of Christ for security.

Yet, like me that morning, being able to see right over the fog, and how bright the day would be, God can see exactly what He wants for our lives and how bright they are going to be. If we hold onto His hand and let Him lead us through the fog, He will lead us out into the bright day, and sometimes He will even lead us to the mountain tops where we can see over the valley and over the fogs of life.

He tells us in Jeremiah 29:11 "For **I** know the **plans I have for you**," declares the Lord, "**plans** to prosper **you** and not to harm **you**, **plans** to give **you** hope and a future." Even if we cannot see clearly, God can.

34

Giving or Receiving

The Bible tells us that "It is more blessed to give than to receive" (Acts 20:35b). There is also a blessing in receiving. After all, if a person is to receive a blessing from giving, there has to be a recipient. It's a strange paradox that in receiving, we give more than we acquire. Once a friend was coming to get some plants but what they didn't realise was that by collecting the plants, they were giving me company, conversation, fellowship. At the time these things were just so important to help me to get up one more time and try again.

Many years ago, we were in a tight financial situation and we had a call to say that there were some funds available for people in need and our names were mentioned. I was told that it was a secret as to who had put our names forward. It was such a blessing. I thanked God over and over for His provision. Unfortunately, a few days later I was asked by the person who had put our names forward if I had had a phone call. I suddenly felt the blessing had been spoilt.

On another occasion, during a drought, we received a bank cheque in the mail, and we had no way of tracing where it came from. We again thanked God for His provision. I know of another family who received a $50 note in the mail, each week, with the address typed so they wouldn't recognise who was sending it, but it was the only money they had to buy groceries with.

God is good and He has good reason to instruct us in Matthew 6:3 "But when thou doest alms (gifts) let not thy left hand know what thy right hand doeth". Just as He says in verse 6b when He is talking about praying "...pray to thy Father which is in secret and thy Father which seeth in secret shall reward thee openly." I think this applies to our giving as well. The reward might be different, but the blessings are greater.

35

God Doesn't Need Me!

I have been following a story written by a very talented young woman. It tells of her faith journey on how God can use her life. One chapter inspired me to think about Abraham. How did God use him? He didn't go out into the world to convert the rest of the world to his God. He just obeyed faithfully, and it was enough for God.

As we read in Hebrews 11:8 "By faith Abraham, when he was called to go out into the place which he should after receive for an inheritance, obeyed and he went out, not knowing whither he went." As a father of only one son, his obedience in being a good father allowed God to fulfil the promise that He had made to Abraham, that of being the father of a great nation.

When I was young with lots of energy and drive, ready to set the world on fire, I was convinced that I had been called to ministry. This conviction did not go away when I met my husband and married. I was certain that my mission in life was to convert my husband's family.

With years of no change, no upfront ministry, I had to realize that God hadn't called me to this sort of ministry. In fact, He taught me many times that He had plenty of people that He wanted to use other than me.

What He had called me to do was be a faithful farmer's wife. This was a very tough call for me. I don't particularly like animals or the routine of farming life. Even as a teenager I had told God that I would never marry a farmer. I can still hear Him giggling at me.

God doesn't need me to work for Him, He just needs me to be obedient.

36

God's Garden

On a couple of consecutive train trips, I noticed some bright flowers growing in what could only be described as dismal circumstances. There were rocks, rubbish, gravel, and steep embankments that would make any growth seem impossible. Yet, these plants were growing happily, giving passers-by something bright to look at, breaking up the otherwise dull scenery. My comments were that, if I had tried to grow such plants in similar places, I would have no hope and yet, here God had planted these flowers with success.

These scenes reminded me of the Parable of the Sower, (Mark 4:3-20) where Jesus talks about the different types of soils and the various results that each soil produces. Interestingly, even though the thorns are said to choke the plants it is not stated that there is absolutely no fruit produced. Looking at those plants during those couple of trips, I was thankful that some good may be produced, even from poor soils. While it isn't going to produce abundantly, the small amounts are able to give blessings to others.

The encouraging thing for me in this is that even if my Christian witness is a struggle and I am sometimes discouraged about how ineffective my life may seem, God has put me where I am so I will be able to grow and be a blessing to those that He directs to pass my way.

2 Corinthians 12:9-10 "But He said to me, My grace is sufficient for you, for my power is made perfect in weakness. Therefore, I will boast all the more gladly about my weakness, so that Christ's power may rest on me. That is why, for Christ's sake I delight in weaknesses, in insults, in hardships, in persecutions, in difficulties. For when I am weak, then I am strong."

37

God's light

In studying the Reformation, I have been excited so far, excited by the number of times during the second darkest time in the world's history (the first being that of the time of Christ's arrival) that there were those occasional voices crying out "by God's grace are we saved through faith." These men lived long before Luther but were still faithful to God who they knew had saved them from their sins by choosing to die on the cross. Yes, these men were lone voices in a world that insisted that salvation came from works and purchases controlled by the church. Yes, they were few and far between and they nearly always paid the price of death for saying so, but what an encouragement to us living now.

If God can keep His light going even in such a dark time in history, how much more should we be assured that He will keep it burning today? How can we lose faith in such a powerful God? A God that keeps His word not only through the ups and downs of the history of Israel and the early church as recorded in the Bible, but also through the continued history of the church since then.

We must continue to tell the world that God is still at work and no matter how dark our existence appears, there is a light, God's light that still says "for by God's grace are we saved through faith and that not of yourselves: it is the gift of God." (Ephesians 2:8).

This simple truth needs to be preached on every occasion possible because one thing is for sure, God has proved His faithfulness this far, and the Book of Revelation tells us He will be faithful to the climax of history.

38

God's Timing

I was reminded this morning, about a Women's group which held a Street Stall many years ago. A Street Stall is a very good way of raising money for small charities. Usually held in the main street of a town, a table is set out loaded with cakes, biscuits, small handicrafts, and good second-hand goods donated by family and friends to be sold. All the proceeds then go to the charity.

In this instance, the town council decided which charity could have what dates as there were a great number of charities wanting to hold such a function. The date given was not the one the ladies would have liked. There was a general discussion and some ladies indicated that a protest to have the decision changed was in order.

The President of the group had had some considerable personal experience with the way God worked. She managed to convince the organisation to go with the set date and to see what God would do.

As it turned out the date that the ladies wanted was wet, windy, and miserable, while the actual day the stall was held was fine and sunny with many more people walking around the street to buy their wares.

There are so many times in our lives when we would like to do certain things at a certain time. Even children often want to be able to do some things long before they are able to or before their parents or society consider it safe for them to do so. In Isaiah 55:8 we read, "For my thoughts are not your thoughts, neither are your ways my ways, saith the Lord."

God himself knows that it is not easy for us to wait upon Him but if we do, He will most likely surprise us with the outcome.

39

Greatness

A great lady, Lady Murdock, known for her charity, hard work, and love for her country, died. At the same time, in another country, a mass killing took place. It appeared this young man wanted to be remembered in history. Lady Diana Spencer and Lady Murdock will both be remembered for their works of charity. History remembers those people who work hard during their lives for the good of mankind.

There is one person who sacrificed His life so that others would be able to live. Jesus Christ did just that. He lived His life, carrying out every day many acts of charity, as we are told in John 21:25. "Jesus did many other things as well. If every one of them were written down, I suppose that even the whole world would not have room for the books that would be written." He then gave up His life on the cross so that all men could be given a way out of eternal death. "For God so loved the world that he gave his one and only Son, that whoever believes in him shall not perish but have eternal life. For God did not send his Son into the world to condemn the world, but to save the world through him." (John 3:16-17).

As I watched the media report on both these people, I found myself wondering why people feel the need to be remembered, if at all, for evil rather than good. Why more people did not take up the banner of charity! Yes, I know that sin dominates our world, but God is stronger, and we should aim, in the strength of Christ, to be remembered for the good we do. The only way for that to happen is for all of us to roll up our sleeves and start.

40

Growing in the Dark

I walked past a garden and looked down at some seedlings that were definitely not looking very robust. The question I asked myself was what had caused them to be such weak plants. The answer was simple: they were growing in the dark! The weeds around them were not only shutting out a large amount of the light but also taking most of the small amount of moisture that was available due to drought conditions.

I realised that as Christians we too can become weak and sickly if we spend too much time in the dark. What this means to me is; if we don't spend enough time in fellowship with other Christians, fail to spend time in prayer, get lazy about studying the word of God or stop communing with the Holy Spirit we too can become spiritually sick. The world is full of weeds, meaning sin abounds all around us. We have to deal with sin at work, in sport, charities that we might work for and we can even find it in our churches.

Making sure that we grow in the full light of God's word is our responsibility. The Bible tells us to "be sober, be vigilant; because your adversary the devil, as a roaring lion, walketh about, seeking whom he may devour." (1 Peter 5:8). This is why when it comes to what we hear being preached we are instructed to, "Ye therefore, beloved seeing ye know these things before, beware lest ye also being led away with the error of the wicked, fall from your own steadfastness, but grow in grace, and in the knowledge of our Lord and Saviour Jesus Christ. To him be glory both now and for ever. Amen." (2 Peter 3:17-18).

41

Have I Done Enough?

I have heard some people express concern about whether they have done enough when it comes to telling others about the love of God.

Once I saw a programme that I thought had a message for a dying family member. I had been praying for them and instinctively I cried out suggesting that they listen to the message. However, they lived miles away and certainly couldn't hear me.

Here are the facts: firstly, I had no idea if this person was even watching television that particular day; secondly, even if they were, I have no idea if they were watching that particular programme; thirdly, I have no idea of what their response would have been if they had been watching.

Will they be in Heaven when I get there? I have no idea. That is completely between God and them. There was no way I could have told this person about the love that God had for them, but God laid it on my heart to pray for them and I did. For the three months that they had left on earth, I prayed for them regardless of my personal feelings. What I do believe, is that God was showing me that He is not limited in the ways that He can bring people to a realization of their sins and to their need for salvation. He didn't need me to talk to them, He could have sent someone else or He could use even a television programme!

"For my thoughts are not your thoughts, neither are your ways my ways, declares the Lord. As the heavens are higher than the earth, so are my ways higher than your ways and my thoughts than your thoughts." (Isaiah 55:8-9).

Sometimes praying just has to be enough.

42

Heaven is a Real Place

I knew a woman who left her abusive relationship, and a Christian social worker who expressed great concern over her safety. As I heard the concerns and the fears in the exchange, I was struck by what seemed to be a lack of confidence in God and the joy of meeting again in Heaven. I was once asked by a Christian friend if I felt guilty about not visiting my parents because I might have regrets if they suddenly died. I later had a conversation with my mother about this and her response was "Don't worry, if we get to Heaven first, we will be waiting for you." With good humour I replied "Great, it might take me 20 years but I will find you."

It is not the first time that I have had this feeling that even Christians are not sure that Heaven is for real. Are we so weighed down by the misery of our world, its worries and the sheer evil that exists, that we have lost sight of Heaven being a real place, where we will have real fellowship with real people that we have known here on Earth?

Jesus told his disciples in John 14:2-3 about the existence of Heaven when He said "In my Father's house are many mansions, if it were not so, I would have told you. I go to prepare a place for you. And if I go and prepare a place for you, I will come again and receive you to Myself; that where I am, there you may be also." John also describes what Heaven will look like in Revelation and even if it all seems too hard to visualise; it still tells us that Heaven is a real place.

43

Here We Go Again

I had to smile. A mother was experiencing one of those moments that we all have had. You know the ones, where you have tried to convince a child that you have their best interests at heart, and they are not convinced at all. Now it was her turn and I just smiled.

It made me wonder though, how many times has God worn a similar smile? I told you! "... that in all things God works for the good of those who love him, who have been called according to His purpose." (Romans 8:28).

There are so many times when we are not convinced that God knows best, just like we were convinced that our parents had no idea of what it was to be young. Yet life is much the same for everyone. Yes, there are differences, using different technologies, having different issues to be concerned about, but ultimately people are made by God and sin makes them react in much the same way as it has since Adam and Eve.

All the way down through history, God has been telling His people that He has their best interests at heart. Still, we insist on doing things our way. "We all, like sheep, have gone astray, each of us has turned to his own way;" (Isaiah 53:6a). It is so easy for us to forget that: "As for God, His way is perfect; the word of the Lord is tried." (2 Samuel 22:31a).

Even as I write, I have to confess I have sometimes doubted/questioned the perfection of God and His ways. I should know better. God has proved over and over, that He really does have my best interests on His heart. With Joseph let's say: "God intended it for good to accomplish what is now being done," Genesis 50:20b.

44

Ignorance is Bliss?

Have you ever had ignored something about a family member and then had it confirmed as true? I did once and it disappointed me greatly. I declared that all those clichés were true. You know the ones: "Ignorance is bliss; what you don't know won't hurt you". But as I walked away, I realised that they are not true.

Just because we don't acknowledge things, doesn't mean that they don't exist. This is what a lot of people do with Jesus. They ignore Him and therefore pretend that He doesn't exist. It's like the old story of a person jumping off a cliff believing that gravity doesn't exist. What happens? They fall to the valley below regardless.

If people continue to ignore God, regardless of what they believe, one day they will have to stand before Him and give an account of what they believed here on earth. In John 3:17-18 it says "For God sent not his Son into the world to condemn the world; but that the world through him might be saved. He that believeth on him is not condemned; but he that believeth not is condemned already, because he hath not believed in the name of the only begotten Son of God." These are tough words, but they are the words of God Himself and one day regardless of how much we ignore them here on earth they will prove to be true when we stand before God on Judgement Day. "And as it is appointed unto men once to die, but after this the judgment." Hebrew 9:27. Jesus came to earth to die for us because He loved us all and ignoring His love will not only hurt Him but also ourselves.

45

International Day for Women

This day is supposed to be a time to recognise the value of women in our society, but we have to learn to value ourselves first before we can be valued by others. I have been known to listen to those other voices so many times in my life. My children yelled, "I hate you" and I heard, "You have done the wrong thing" not "I'm just throwing a tantrum." One would burst into tears and I would hear, "You are hurting me", not, "I don't like the rules". I clearly remember the first time I gave myself credit for being a good mum (I had been a mum for many years by then). It came about when another woman, who I thought, and, society told me, was better qualified to understand the needs of my child than I was, said she didn't want to care for my child after only one night. I had looked after my child for years and not once had I said that I didn't want them.

There is so little positive information circulating about women. Television adverts make women into blonde sex symbols so many times that the only thing you can do is switch off or these messages will sink in. Unfortunately, these messages sink into your children's heads, both boys and girls. In order to help our children, we need to make sure that we do not listen to the voices out there, the ones that say women are just a decoration, or they only get to the top by being bullies.

Yes, God made us out of the rib of Adam, but He didn't make us to be put down. He made us to be a "helpmate" - someone that could walk beside our man, talk to our man, and had a soul that was the same as a man's. That is why he couldn't find a companion amongst the animals. They didn't share the same soul as he had. (Genesis 2:18-24).

It is easy to get discouraged when all those other voices tell you that you are not doing enough, the wrong thing, or you are not capable. God made you! You are made in His image and He has a plan for your life regardless of whether you are married, a single mum, or just single. He understands your struggles, your needs, your dreams, and your hopes.

Ladies, today is not really International Day for Women - that is just a tag that has been placed on March 8th each year. International Day for women is a 365 day exercise, an exercise in which we should celebrate our strengths, our abilities to carry on in the face of adversity, band together and help each other, pray for each other, teach our children both male and female that women are equal, need respect and they are considered equal by Christ. Let us appreciate what we have and strive to gain what we have for those that are not fortunate enough to have their basic rights respected.

46

Jigsaw

The jigsaw of my life was laid out in pieces. The situation was one that had been a matter of prayer for a few weeks and the state of affairs did not seem to be any closer to being resolved. In fact, the mystery surrounding the circumstances was just getting deeper and deeper. It seemed like a puzzle where all the pieces look pretty much the same in colour and shape and as you try each piece that looks as if it will fit, you find that it is just not quite right.

Through tears I prayed, "Oh Lord, the pieces are all laid out and you know which ones belong where. We could always force the pieces into the picture, but I really want this picture to be your creation. Give me the patience, strengthen my faith and help me to stand back and let you fit this position into your great scheme."

Romans 8:25 says "But if we hope for that we see not, then do we with patience wait for it." I had no idea what plan God had in mind for us and I still cannot see the big picture, but I have to wait uncomplainingly. Don't get me wrong, this is not easy for me to do. I also know that God has a good plan for me.

He could be waiting for someone else to make a decision to follow His lead. Maybe that person's decision is the pivot that the plan works on. It is very hard to get our heads around the fact that we all fit together in such a way, but we do. We are all members of one body (1 Corinthians 12:14) and if one-part stops working then the whole body has a problem. Is your part working?

47

Know What we Ask For!

As a child many years ago, I heard about how a mother's young adult son had sustained horrific injuries in an accident. The doctors told her that he would die. She begged God to let her son live. God answered her prayers and she spent the next 20 years begging God to let her son die. Why? God had let her son live but his quality of life as a result of the injuries sustained was such that his mother realised that God had had a more merciful answer in the first place.

There are times when we pray, asking God for specific things, and we have no idea what we are asking. Many times, I have caught myself asking God for something in particular and realising later that He has given me exactly what I asked for, not what was my real desire. For instance, I once asked for a normal family, only to discover that my heart's desire of normal was very different to what was actually a normal family in today's society. On other occasions God has given me the desire of my heart. Had He given me what I actually asked for, I would have been in a far more difficult situation that I had been before. It is only in hindsight that I realised just how careless those prayers were.

Jesus rebukes the Mother of James and John when she asks Him to allow one son to sit on His right side and the other on His left. (Matthew 20:20-28) "Ye know not what ye ask." He says and continues to ask.

"Are ye able to drink of the cup that I shall drink of and to be baptized with the baptism that I am baptized with?" (verse 22).

Matthew 6:33 tells us that "But seek ye first the kingdom of God, and His righteousness: and all these things shall be added unto you."

48

Kookaburra Sing

One morning I could hear the kookaburras laughing outside. They were singing their hearts out. As this was during a period when there had been more than enough rain for everyone, my first depressing thought was, "It's most likely going to rain again." As they continued to sing it really began to sound like they were just happy to be alive.

If they are able to predict rain in the way that the myths say, then I'm sure they were not looking forward to more rain coming either. Maybe their singing helps them feel better about the bad weather that they are predicting.

When you think of all the songs that King David wrote, he must have sung a lot for no particular reason. As I stop to actually think about this, I realized that there probably times when he just started singing to help him feel better about the storms of life that were in his pathway.

Looking at how many Psalms start out with concerns and worries and end in praises to God it would appear that it worked on many occasions and God is trying to tell me something about how to deal with the lows in my life.

Psalm 132 starts with, "Lord, remember David, and all his afflictions" and he continues to list his concerns about what is happening until verse 11 when he remembers the promises that God has given to him and the tone changes. "The Lord hath sworn in truth unto David; he will not turn from it; of the fruit of thy body will I set upon thy throne."

Remembering how faithful God is will lift my focus from the doldrums to the God of power and light and then I really do feel like singing at top of my voice.

49

Left Behind

We were discussing a tragedy, and someone made the comment, "Death doesn't happen to you but to those that you leave behind." At first, I wasn't sure but as I thought about it later, I found to some degree this comment was right. Once we die, we have embarked on our eternal journey. We understand the error of our ways, where we messed up and that the justice of God is true and perfect. It means therefore that the consequences of our choices are also understood and accepted as being correct. This we glean from the story of the rich man and Lazarus (Luke 16:19-31). The rich man knew that he was in the place that he should have been because of the way he had lived his life on earth. Lazarus, while it is not stated in the story has to have been a faithful servant and goes to Heaven. God's justice was perfect. In verse 27 and 28, the rich man pleads with Peter to send Lazarus to his brothers to make sure that they know about what happens after they die.

While we might be sure of our destination while we are still here, we often live with those constant questions of why, what, and how. Why did this happen? Why now? What really happened? What are we going to do now? What can we do to stop this happening again? What didn't we do that we should have done? How are we going to manage? How do we keep going? The questions are endless and often there are no simple answers.

No matter what our circumstances are, God promises that if we ask Him, He will give us the strength to carry on. Paul writes in Philippians 4:13, "I can do all things through Christ which strengtheneth me." We will be able to say the same when we call on the name of Christ.

50

Lessons from my Woodbox

One winter I wanted to clean up the wood heap, which hadn't been sorted for several years.

This meant, though, that the wood supply was reduced to almost nothing. There came a time when there was very little left at the wood heap. Anticipating some predicted rain and accompanying cold snap, I went in search of some pieces that could be found lying around in a paddock. I managed to fill a wheelbarrow with some very scrappy, odd-looking pieces that did not look like they would burn well. What I discovered, however, was that these odd-looking, ugly pieces of wood burned faster and hotter than the nice neat pieces that I was used to using.

So, what lessons did God teach me:

1. If we are left lying around in the paddock, we are no use to anyone. Now I know that the wood did not have a choice about where it was left but we do! We have a choice - are we going to allow God to use us or are we going to ignore His call on our lives?

2. It doesn't matter what we look like to people around us, if we allow God to use us, He will do great things with us. Yes, the wood looked ugly and lumpy and didn't fit in the woodbox neatly. It is how God uses us that is important. If you find it hard for you to fit in, don't let it get you down, it may well mean that God will probably achieve more through you!

3. When my woodbox was filled with the neatly split wood, my stove did not produce as much heat as I would have liked,

and it took much longer to cook. Many of us would like our churches, small groups, and organisations to be filled with a certain category of people. They are easier to deal with as they fit into our plans and programs better. I suspect that these sorts of organizations may only smoulder for God instead of being on fire for Him.

In Matthew Chapter 22 Jesus tells a parable about a king who invites all the respectable people to a feast. However, they decide that they don't want to come to the king's table. In the end, in order to have a feast at all, the king sends his servants out to the highways and invited all those who did not fit into the social set of the king. Our responsibility is to look to Him and allow Him to use us for His glory.

51

Let Go and Let God

With the evenings growing cooler the job of lighting the fuel stove to provide some warmth to the kitchen fell to me. While it was not really important that it was going it was just nice to have the extra heat and some savings on the electricity bill. A few days after we had decided to start lighting the stove, I tried to start it but it wasn't in the mood to go (if a stove can have a mood). I was busy with a lot of other things during the day and only made a few half-hearted attempts to get it going.

About four o'clock the fire suddenly burst into life without my assistance. As I said a quiet thank you to God, strangely I was reminded of something that I had read a long time ago. If you have a problem, leave it alone for three days. Two things will probably happen. Either a solution will present itself or the problem will go away and not need a solution. In the meantime, you have reduced your stress levels for the three days. Of course, if the problem still exists then it's time to ask God for His solution.

1 John 5:14-15 tells us, "This is the confidence we have in approaching God: that if we ask anything according to His will, He hears us. And if we know that He hears us – whatever we ask – we know that we have what we asked of Him." Isaiah 65:24 tells us that, "Before they call, I will answer; while they are still speaking I will hear."

So, I am reminded not to worry about a problem. I'm reminded to let go for three days and then if need be, let God deal with it.

52

Letting Go

As many of my friends face the marriages of the children, it is interesting to see their reactions. Some are happy, others were guarded, and some just horrified. Of course, as usual, when these occasions come up, the memories of our own wedding come flooding back. There were stresses and disappointments. Misunderstandings that caused problems that had to be sorted. I realize that there are great expectations on both sides. Parents want the best for their children and find it hard to let go. I never understood how my parents felt about my own marriage until my daughter announced that she was getting married. There are fears that just come flooding in to be faced.

As I thought about this whole process it occurred to me that each party probably needs to lower their expectations. Life is very real and tough. As hard as it is, we must allow our children to learn their own lessons with their choice of husband/wife. We have to trust God to teach them what He wants and take them on the journey that He has for them. Children need to realize life will be tough. This letting go of your child was also brought home to me very vividly when another one of my children's marriages broke down. God clearly told me one night, that they were no longer mine, they were His and I had to trust Him to look after them.

God tells us that the natural outcome of life is that a child will leave their parents, "For this reason a man will leave his father and mother ....." Genesis 2:24a. It's hard but we can trust God to look after our children.

53

Life Giving Water

I look out at the paddocks that are bare and barren from the effects of a long drought. There appears to be no life left in them at all. Yet I know in my heart that as soon as the rain comes, not even lots of rain, life will spring up again. It will take time but it will come. Some paddocks will have to be sown with new seed but again life will return.

These paddocks are just like some people. They have been dried up, damaged and left poor in spirit. It may be from the side effects of sin, (either their own or those of others) illness or just having their priorities in the wrong place. Yet when God enters their life and showers them with His love, care, and Holy Spirit they too will spring into life. A life that will give glory to Him, a life that will serve Him with faithfulness that is born out of gratefulness to God.

Jesus offered the Samaritan women living water. (John 4:1-42). He offers the same water to each of us. Water, that once we drink it, will flow constantly through our lives to those around us. In order for us to be able to have this water, we must, however, come to Jesus and ask Him to cleanse us of all our sins. John 5:24 tells us: "Verily, Verily, I say unto you. He that heareth my word and believeth on Him that sent me hath everlasting life and shall not come into condemnation; but is passed from death unto life."

God will send His life-giving rain for the paddocks in His own time, but will you accept His life-giving water now because God does tell us that the Day of Salvation is now (2 Corinthians 6:2).

54

Life's Road

On yet another road trip, I travelled along some very damaged stretches. There had been so much wind, rain and in some cases flood water that the roads were potholed and broken. As I drove along, trying to avoid the potholes, it occurred to me that these roads could represent my life. We all have to face the storms of life and no, we cannot avoid the damage that they will do to us.

Driving past workmen, who were fixing parts of the road in the rain, I was encouraged to remember that God would be out in all weathers patching my life's storm damage as well. Yes, it would look scarred and battered but it would still be a good thing, just like that road that I was travelling along was still good, it would get me to where I was going. However, not the entire road had been damaged, presumably because the foundations of the road were strong and built properly by the builders.

If therefore, God has made me in His image and that is good, then when the storms of life come and rage against me, because of the foundations that my life is based on, I will be able to withstand the fury. They may damage some things but not break me completely.

In Matthew 7:24-27 Jesus describes people who listen to Him and have a relationship with Him as being wise and like those that build their house on a rock foundation. Foolish people are described as building their houses on sand. Regardless of what we are building, houses, roads, or lives, they all need to be built on a solid foundation and for our lives the only foundation that is solid enough for eternity is Christ.

55

Life's Storybook

A particular chapter of my life had come to an end. It was finished! As I waited to find out what was in store for me next, I got to thinking that life is just like a story. It is sometimes said that our lives are made up of various chapters. That made me think about how a book has many chapters but the last one is the one that finishes the story. I then realised that, yes, while our lives might be like a story in a book there is one very big difference. Our last chapter will go on for eternity!

Revelation 21 and 22:1-5 tells us something of what that chapter will be like for those of us who have faith in Jesus and have had our sins forgiven. On the other hand, we read in Matthew 8:12, Matthew 22:13 and Revelation 20: 11-15 of the consequences for those who do not have their names written in the Book of Life.

Every person will have a different story written about them but there will only be one of two last chapters for all of us. One chapter will be our lives spent eternally in Heaven and the other will be eternity in Hell. All of us still have unfinished stories, chapters that are still to be written. It depends on how we write those chapters as to which closing chapter will be the last in our story.

If you are reading this, you are still living and still have time. The pages of your book are still clean, waiting to be written on. How your story continues determines the final chapter for your life. Choose Jesus and Heaven will be the final destination, Ignore Him and Hell is inevitable. Which final chapter will be yours?

56

Light Bulb Moments

I was driving into town, early one morning, when the windscreen fogged up, making it hard to see. The air conditioner was switched on. My passenger and I watched in amazement as the windscreen almost instantly cleared. In fact, you could see the moisture drying off the glass. Clear vision restored, I thought about those moments in my life when suddenly something that God wanted me to understand, finally broke through and I got it.

I am reminded of those times when you go looking for something, that you know is around somewhere and you just don't seem to be able to put your hand on it. Yet eventually, in my case, usually after I prayed and asked God to open my eyes so I can see what it is that I am looking for, it is found and I'm left wondering how on earth I walked past it so many times and didn't see it.

I remembered a moment in the Bible when two people had what we call a "Light Bulb Moment". Moments when it is as if the light has been turned on and something made sense. It was the two disciples walking to Emmaus. In Luke 24:13-35 verse 31 says "Then their eyes were opened and they recognized him". Sometimes regardless of how many times we have read a particular passage, we suddenly get some new inspiration from it. John 16:13 says: "But when He, the Spirit of truth, comes, He will guide you into all truth. He will not speak on his own; he will speak only what he hears, and he will tell you what is yet to come."

I pray that I will be willing to find some new truth each day, regardless of how it comes.

57

Looking a Gift Horse in the Mouth

I was thinking about a story in which a husband wanted to improve the house. The house they were living in had no proper bathroom. His first child was on the way and he felt that a proper bathroom was warranted. His wife's response was, "If it was good enough for my mother then it's good enough for me." Yes, I can hear the men saying "Wow" and the women saying "What!" Why would either of these people look such a gift horse in the mouth and not accept?

But think about this. What is the greatest gift ever given to the human race that is turned down nearly every day by hundreds of people? Romans 3:23 tells us that, "For all have sinned and fall short of the glory of God," and therefore the one gift that can improve any person's life, would be the forgiveness of their sins. How many people do you know, who say, "I'm ok, I live a good life, what needs to be improved or forgiven?"

So, what is the process involved in fixing this problem as stated in the Romans 3:23? Firstly, we need to acknowledge that we have sinned, "Wherefore, as by one man sin entered into the world, and death by sin; and so death passed upon all men, for that all have sinned." (Romans 5:12). Believe that Jesus will forgive you for your sins and confess them to Him. "If we confess our sins, he is faithful and just to forgive us our sins, and to cleanse us from all unrighteousness." (1 John 1:9).

From that point, you need to continue to read your Bible, have fellowship with other Christians and continue to grow in Christ.

First, though, are you ignoring the greatest gift ever given?

58

Looking Back

I knew of a church that went through a stage of being so proud of its history. It ended up looking back for so long that it began failing to meet, not only the needs of its own church community but also the needs of the non-Christian community around it.

Thinking about this, I realised that we often sit in church, facing what we regard as the front of the church. It is in fact the back of the church. We enter by the front door and face the back where we hear the word of God preached from the pulpit. This particular church had heard the word of God preached for many years and while they were concentrating on their history, they forgot that they needed to turn around and walk back out the front door, which leads to all the opportunities for ministry. Those ministries include Sunday school, Pastoral Care, SRE in Schools and Evangelism.

What is easy to forget is that the reason we go to church is to be equipped to reach sinners for Christ.

In Matthew 28:18-20 we read, "And Jesus came and spake unto them saying. All power is given unto me in heaven and on earth. Go ye therefore and teach all nations, baptizing them in the name of the Father, and of the Son, and of the Holy Ghost: Teaching them to observe all things whatsoever I have commanded you and Lo, I am with you always, even unto the end of the world. Amen."

It's a tough thing to do but we need to take Him at His word and get out of our comfortable seats, stop looking back, march out of the doors and start bringing people to an understanding of His love for them.

59

Loudly Proclaim

Once we were babysitting or rather "cat sitting" a cat for a friend for a couple of weeks while they got themselves settled into a new place. When the cat was released from its box, it bolted and went into hiding. I was the only person to even get some idea of where it was hiding. I left some food out in the vicinity of where I thought it was camped out in order to try and make sure that it wouldn't starve, but I was unsure whether it was actually eating the food or if the food was being devoured by the other pets that were residents of our place. The night the owner of this cat returned, the cat not only came out of hiding, but loudly voiced its pleasure at the owner's arrival. At about 1.30AM, I woke and heard the cat still going on at full volume, telling all cats in hearing distance "my owner is back, she still loves me, she hasn't forgotten me," (I guess).

As I listened, I thought it's just like us when we have a close relationship with Jesus. We tell the whole world that Jesus has come, Jesus has saved us, and Jesus loves not only us but the entire human race. If there is distance between us and God because of sin, we go quiet, we hide, just as Adam and Eve did in the Garden of Eden (Genesis 3:8): "And they heard the voice the Lord God walking in the garden in the cool of the day, and Adam and his wife hid themselves from the presence of the Lord God amongst the trees of the garden.".

Once our relationship with God has been restored because we have accepted the gift of salvation that was made available to us through Christ's death on the cross and His resurrection, then we should be happy to tell all who will listen, what a wonderful thing it is that has happened. Luke 24:46-48 says "And (Jesus) said unto them, thus it is written and thus it behoved Christ to suffer and to rise from the dead the third day: and that repentance and remission of sins should be preached in his name among all nations beginning at Jerusalem. And ye are witnesses of these things."

It is a wonderful thing to be in a close relationship with Christ. Let all of us who have the privilege, loudly proclaim it to the rest of the world, that they too can learn how they can have such an honour.

60

Loving Us

The young mum is in tears. Her children have hurt her once again. As I listen, memories flood back. How many times did my children do the same thing to me? One of the toughest jobs a parent has to do is love their children unconditionally. As I struggle to comfort, I remember that God our Father has loved humanity since the beginning of time, unconditionally. How many people hurt Him by doing things the way they wanted do, ignoring Him and trying to destroy His Son and those that do love Him.

Unconditional love, says: I have your best interests at heart, even if you don't like the things you have to do, to develop the skills that you need to survive when I am no longer able to do things for you. I love you no matter how hard you push me away. You can even hate me, but I still will want all this for you.

Therefore God, no matter how much sin we carry, sent Jesus to die on the Cross for us. "For God so loved the world that He sent His one and only Son, that whoever believes in Him shall not perish but have eternal life." (John 3:16). It is why after Jesus returned to Heaven, He sent the Holy Spirit to be our interpreter and our counsellor, "And I will ask the Father, and He will give you another to be with you forever," John 14:16 says, "Whenever you are arrested and brought to trial, do not worry beforehand about what to say. Just say whatever is given you at the time, for it is not you speaking, but the Holy Spirit." (Mark 13:11).

Every time someone hurts you, regardless of who they are, family or stranger, remember Jesus is hurt too and understands.

61

Makeover

We had a table made of cheap painted chipboard which was showing the damage of the years of use or abuse that had been inflicted on it. We decided that we would like to use it outside for occasional meals in the shade of our verandah. It was obvious that the weather would destroy it even more and make it useless unless something was done. My son set about removing the old tabletop and put together a new, hardwood timber one. He was cutting, screwing, and hammering things into place. Our daughter then got to work, sanding, staining, and varnishing to protect the new top from the weather.

As I watched all the hard work that went into this makeover, I thought about how God will do the same for all of us if we would only let Him.

In 2 Corinthians 5:17 we read "Therefore if any man be in Christ, he is a new creature: old things are passed away; behold, all things are become new." Ephesians also tells us in 4:23 "And be renewed in the spirit of your mind; and that ye put on the new man, which after God is created in righteousness and true holiness. Wherefore putting away lying, speak every man truth with his neighbour; for we are members one of another. Be ye angry, and sin not; let not the sun go down upon your wrath; neither give place to the devil."

God shows us what is wrong with our lives and what needs to be done, and then with His forgiveness and strength, we are able to develop a new life that will give glory to our Heavenly Father and ultimately see us praising God in Heaven for eternity.

62

Missed Opportunities

I had to get up one morning considerably earlier than normal. As I was already up, I decided to stoke up the heater as the day was looking like being a bit chilly. It brought to mind a family story. In the very early hours of the morning after my Great Grandfather's conversion at a campfire during the night, he wanted spiritual counsel from a Minister of a church in town. He rode his horse past each Denomination's home and checked their chimneys to see if the occupants were up yet. If there was no smoke it meant that the fires had not been stirred into life and therefore the family was still in bed. There was smoke coming out of only one chimney that morning. The Salvation Army Officer had that morning risen and stirred his fire. The knock on the door was no doubt a surprise and maybe a little daunting. I think I would be saying "What can anyone want at this hour of the morning". This man joined the Salvation Army and four generations have served the church in one form or other.

It makes me wonder how many opportunities I have missed just because I was a little slow to get moving on any project or course of action.

In Psalm 63:1 David prays to God: "O God, thou art my God; early will I seek thee: my soul thirsteth for thee, my flesh longeth for thee in a dry and thirsty land, where no water is." Also, in Proverbs 8:17 we read "I love them that love me and those that seek me early shall find me."

I know that in my Great grandfathers' case, it wouldn't have mattered who was up that morning in regard to his salvation but it would have made a big difference to where he served His Lord. That Salvation Army Officer had no idea just how many people's lives he was going to affect that morning. I understand that it is much easier to put something off than to get up and get on with it and we have no way of knowing how many lives will be affected by what we do or don't do. I pray that I will be careful about what I put off in the future.

63

Missing Ingredient

I cooked some muffins one day and was surprised when I had one that they didn't taste as nice as usual. They were definitely still edible, just not as enjoyable as I would like. That could be a good thing of course; I would not eat them as fast as I normally would. It took some time for me to remember that I had actually forgotten to put in one ingredient. The honey was still in the cupboard.

How much was this like our lives? They can look normal, the muffins did. We can act as if nothing was wrong, the muffins still rose properly. But with one ingredient missing, things are just not quite right. The muffins tasted unpleasant!

I was thinking about how so many people live, act, and look like life is great, but without Christ in their lives, things are not quite right, even if they won't admit it.

In Luke 16:19-31 we read about a man who had a great life on earth, he was rich and about the only thing that annoyed him was a beggar at his gate by the name of Lazarus. When it came to eternity however, the tables were turned on him. Hell, which is where he ended up, was all bad. Why? The reason was that he had ignored God, but Lazarus whom he had also ignored, enjoyed eternity in Heaven because God was a part of his life.

Jesus says: I am the way, the truth and the life, no one comes to the Father except through me." Without Christ in their lives, so many people are going to find that eternity is going to be very miserable because of one missing ingredient – JESUS.

64

Mobile Phones and the Bible

Like most families, we have a number of mobile phones in our home. There are different models with different functions. Mine is used a lot and members of my family ring me frequently with instructions or requests. I'm the first to admit that I don't use all the functions that my phone is capable of carrying out, unlike my children who use many of their phone's functions. However, there is one phone which is still in its box. There is nothing wrong with the phone, but it sits there not being used. So, what do these mobile phones have to do with a Bible?

Some people have a Bible that they study and use every day, taking from it, instructions from God and learning how He would like them to live. Other people read only selected sections of it, sometimes not really taking in what they are reading. There are those, however, who have a Bible which sits on the shelf, doing nothing.

Like the mobile phone, the more we learn how to use the Bible to find out how God wants us to live and change us, the greater amount of help it will be in our lives. If, however, it sits on the shelf, while there is nothing wrong with what it can do, it will be useless.

65

Movement

Do you remember the Christmas poem that says, "T'was the night before Christmas and all through the house, not a creature was stirring, not even a mouse?" Well, one morning I woke to such a house. It was so quiet, even the chooks seemed to be settled. The windows were closed against what little breeze may have been stirring outside. It was just so silent, a bit like my life, still, silent and going nowhere. When I rolled over on to my back, I happened to look up at one of my wind chimes hanging from the ceiling. It was moving! I even checked out the other chimes in the room and they were still. I watched and asked God what He was trying to tell me. The answer that came was, you think your life is not going anywhere but even if you cannot see it or hear it, I am moving something at my command.

I was reminded of the story of Elijah and his encounter with God. (1 Kings 19:9-18) Elijah wants God to speak to him, but His voice is neither in the wind nor the earthquake (verse 11). Elijah did not hear the voice of God in the fire but as a still small voice (verse 12).

In a world that is noisier than ever, louder than it needs to be and much faster than it should be, God wants us to take time out to listen to His quiet voice. Yes, we might want God to speak to us loudly so we can hear Him over the busyness of life but more than ever we need to stop and quietly listen to what He has to say.

Will you stop and listen to Him today?

66

My Son

My youngest son was a precocious child. He had an insatiable thirst for knowledge and a determination that is rare. When he was learning to read, he would ask anybody who was handy what a road sign said or what words were on billboards. If you took him shopping and we couldn't find an item, it was him that would just say, "I'll go and ask someone", and off he would go and find a staff member (they had uniforms) and we would soon know if the product was somewhere else other than where we were looking, or just sold out. His confidence amazed me at times. This meant though that there were times when he got hurt as he approached adults who did not have the time or energy to assist him.

As he grew into the teenage phase, he lost that childlike faith and oomph, but I pray that as an adult he will find a new maturity that will see him again find that get-up-and-go.

In the church we see this process happen even in the lives of new converts. Young Christians often start out with that same insatiable thirst for knowledge and determination and you see them getting things done because they will not take "NO" for an answer, from people or from God. Yes, they get hurt, sometimes very hurt and this knocks their confidence around, sometimes so much that they can lose their vitality. They in effect became teenagers. Yet, with all my studies of the bible I have never ever seen the word "teenager" mentioned. Children are mentioned and we grow into adults. "When I was a child, I spake as a child, I understood as a child, I thought as a child; but when I became a man, I put away childish things." 1 Corinthians 13:11.

Let's not be teenagers when it comes to trusting and working for God.

67

Networking

One morning, we discovered a lost dog at our place. He was a loved pet of someone that lived quite a distance from our property. In order to find the owner, we ended up using the Facebook network. I placed the photo on my page and asked my friends to share it in order to get the message out to as many people as I could. All day we waited for someone to call and nothing happened. My son came home, and he placed the photo on his page and we waited some more.

Later that night, my son did receive some messages from friends that he went to school with, telling him that it looked as if we had found their auntie's dog. Then the call from the owner came. They made arrangements to collect the dog in the morning.

While I thought about the story behind this situation, I realised that while it was a good example of how God will rescue us in an instant, it was also a good example of our responsibility to reach out to others and tell them about the love the Lord of God has for each of us.

Romans 10:15 says, "And how shall they preach, except they be sent as it is written. How beautiful are the feet of them that preach the gospel of peace, and bring glad tidings of good things!"

I realised that it sometimes takes a great network of people to get the message to those that God wants to reach. Those people may not be ready to listen the first time the message is preached but we are not to give up because eventually, they will hear that God loves them and has a plan for them.

68

None of Your Business

I had been listening to a series of sermons on the ministry of the Holy Spirit. Unintentionally it was implied that the Holy Spirit had not been working in our Church or my life and yes, I was taking it personally. Sitting through one particular sermon, I screamed at God, asking Him to show the preacher how much the Holy Spirit had worked in my life over the many years that I had had that very personal relationship with Him. God just screamed back, "It's none of his business!"

Thinking about this later I realised that I was just like Herod who wanted Jesus to do a miracle (Luke 23:8). The Holy Spirit has been sent to help us (John 14:16) and yes there will be times when He will have to do something spectacular to help us but usually, He will be there to give us the right words to say to someone in grief or witness to a non-Christian who needs to know that God died for them on the cross. When asked, He will help a preacher say the right words each Sunday, fifty-two weeks a year, at funerals, weddings, and baptisms.

I don't believe that the Holy Spirit is a showoff. He is not going to perform just so people can look at Him. Just like Jesus, the glory must go to the Father; "Jesus answered, I have not a devil; but I honour my Father and you do dishonour me. And I seek not mine own glory; there is one that seeketh and judgeth." (John 8:49-50). The main task is to teach us what the Word of God means for each of us and, as in the great commission (Mathew 28:19-20), lead us out into the world to make disciples.

69

Order

During a clean-up, I was having trouble convincing my family that it was really necessary. It had been such a long time since I had had one that I think they thought I had gone mad. It did get me thinking though about the old saying: Cleanliness is next to Godliness. The thing about cleanliness is that it means keeping everything in its right place and having some sort of routine that keeps putting things in order.

After all I'm so glad that God is a God of order. How strange it would be if we woke up today to find that today was Summer but when we woke up tomorrow it might be Winter or Autumn or even Spring. What if we woke to find that the sun decided not to rise today, and the moon was up all day instead or even that there was no light at all for the day? Yes, we can laugh but these things don't happen because God has put them in place and ordered that their routine be the same way each and every day.

So, what does this do with our lives? It means that while variety is a good thing there also needs to be a routine and order to our lives. After all, God instructs us through His word to pray constantly as in 1 Thessalonians 5:17, "Pray without ceasing." He also instructs us to meet together with other Christians: "Not forsaking the assembling of ourselves together, as the manner of some is; but exhorting one another and so much the more, as ye see the day approaching." Hebrews 10:25.

70

Passing the Buck

It was one of those rare occasions when there was a couple of our children home for a meal. Normally, these days, it's just my husband and me for dinner. It is our custom to say "Grace", thanking God for our meal. Normally when it's just myself and my husband it's done by whoever has not put the meal together. This night, there was some discussion about whose turn it was to give thanks. It seemed that everyone in the room felt that it was someone else's duty to thank God for what we were about to eat. After several attempts to pass the buck, as we call it in Australia, my son agreed to say grace.

Thinking about this later, I wondered how many times God says, "Get someone else to go and make disciples?" rather than "...Go ye into all the world and preach the gospel to every creature." (Mark 16: 15). Did He tell Peter to get someone else to feed His sheep? No "...He saith unto him Feed my Sheep." (John 21:16). Now you can prove me wrong if you like but I can't find it.

Each of us will have a different job to do for the Lord and He does have a different plan for each of us! There is no getting away from the fact that we are to carry out those plans ourselves, not in our own strength of course but we cannot pass the buck to anyone else. If we carry on faithfully, then one day we will be able to stand before God our Father and hear Him say "....Blessed are the dead which die in the Lord for henceforth: yea, saith the Spirit that they may rest from their labours and their works do follow them." Revelation 14:13.

71

Ploughing

One Sunday morning, we sang a hymn which goes "Sing we the King who is coming to reign". As we sang "Sword shall be ploughshares, when Jesus is King", I was struck by the truth of this line. During the week, we had had both a wonderful and terrible display of pastoral care in the middle of a devastating drought that was draining us emotionally to the point of exhaustion. Yet while we sang this song, I realised that the phrase that said, "Jesus is King" was the defining difference in the results.

In the first instance, the minister came to visit. He saw our problem firsthand, even though he could do absolutely nothing to meet our greatest need, rain. He treated us with respect, love, and care. He took a great interest in the other things that were going on in our lives. Talking about these things gave us something else to focus on, other than the horrible conditions of our paddocks which we were still looking at, as we spoke. For that hour we were able to forget the drought and share the other things that were important to us generally but get pushed into the background in times of stress.

In the second instance, people were required to go to a central meeting point. They were lectured on what they should and should not do and told that other people (younger than themselves) knew what to do in drought better than they did.

What a contrast! One used a ploughshare, the other a sword. In Isaiah 2:2-4 the Bible talks about how when Jesus is King, harmony will exist between humans instead of disharmony. We often put this into a future context but on that Sunday morning, I realised that when Jesus is King in our lives, it will exist now.

72

Preacher's Kid

As a child, I was so proud of my father. He was a preacher! As far as I was concerned, he stood right up there along with Peter and Paul, preaching the Word of God. With age, I came to realise that my mental statue of my father had feet of clay. He was, after all, completely human. While I'm not certain if it was because we never stayed in any one place for long, or my parent's diligence, I somehow got the message that my father was only a preacher. No church and no one denomination have it entirely right. They are and always will be human institutions, with flaws as a result of that humanness.

It is easy to admire any preacher too much. Paul addressed this problem even with the early church in Corinth, "What I mean is this: One of you says, "I follow Paul"; another, "I follow Apollos"; another, "I follow Cephas"; still another "I follow Christ." Is Christ divided? Was Paul crucified for you? Were you baptised into the name of Paul?" (1 Corinthians 1:12-13). Dead or alive, no one is the head of any church except CHRIST.

According to our Apostles' Creed, we believe in "The holy Catholic Church" which simply means a Universal Church, a church that has only one head. I am only just beginning to see what a blessing it was to have had such a childhood and I am grateful to God that He taught me who the real head of His church is.

73

Pushing the Limits

I was minding a grandson when he was learning to walk. He was at that stage where he was able to stand by himself but needed support to actually walk. On this particular day, he was using a dining room chair, pushing it in front of him. Now, this house has a couple of steps leading down into a sunken lounge room. I knew that if he was crawling around, he could negotiate up and down these steps. I watched him pushing the chair around the dining room. However, it was not long before he was headed for the stairs. Because the chair was in front of him, he had no idea where he was going, but I did. In response to the danger that was ahead of him, I stood up and put enough force on the chair to prevent the perceived danger from becoming a reality. Of course, the child's response was to push as hard as he could in order to try and keep going in the direction that he had started in. When that didn't work, the next strategy was to get cranky and throw a tantrum. So, the battle of wills continued, until he decided with a little encouragement that a safer direction was a good plan. Once he was moving again, the tantrums stopped and progress was made and of course, he was saved from falling down the stairs.

Again, I was reminded of a number of times when I have wanted to do something, only to find that there is a force preventing me from moving forward. That force, of course, was God saying, 'this is not where I want you to go'. In Colossians 2:2-3 we find "....Christ in whom are hidden all the treasures of wisdom and knowledge."

74

Routine

I was catching up in the garden after being away for a few weeks. As I was getting rid of some rubbish, I had a smug thought: "I'll have this finished soon and then I can stop." As I turned around and looked at my yard on the way back, I realized two things. One, that gardening never stops and if I did it would only get out of control again. Secondly, the only way I was ever going to be able to stay on top of the workload that keeps it under control was to develop a routine that made sure work was being done on a regular basis.

That got me thinking about our Christian lives and how we need a routine of Bible Study and prayer to make sure that the garden of our "Spiritual Life" is kept neat and tidy. There have been times when "being away" spiritually has meant that my circumstances have overwhelmed me and the only way to cope with the mess that I found myself in was to come home to God and rely on Him to help me through whatever consequences resulted.

1 Thessalonians 5:17 tells us to "pray continually;" we cannot do that if we do not have a routine of talking to Jesus. A routine may include praying while we are washing the dishes, gardening, driving in the car or on our knees before we go to bed. Talking to God constantly will ensure that those times of stress will be lower because we are close to Him.

Do you have a routine of praying continually?

75

Scaffolding

While working away, some people decided that a roof on a two-story building needed to be fixed. In order to make sure that the workers were safe there was a huge amount of scaffolding erected so that they were able to reach the roof safely, which is a good thing. Sometimes scaffolding is used to support the actual structure if the foundations are not very sound.

In church life, I think it is easy to erect such scaffolding. How? Many programs are designed to bring more members into our churches but if the Church's foundations are based on Jesus Christ, we won't need many of them. When we continue to give glory to God and tell others about Him, He will ensure that people's hearts are challenged, and the Holy Spirit will go to work changing hearts and lives. The other problem with programs is that many hours are wasted making sure that the politics within the groups are working. This means we are kept busy and distracted from the real job that God wants us to do.

Jesus says, "But I, when I am lifted up from the earth, will draw all men to myself", (John 12:32). Yes, it tells us about the death of Jesus, but it reminds us that God is greater than any of us. It is easy to think that we are the only means that God can use and while He wants us to be of assistance it is also a bit arrogant.

When we are thinking about developing programs and ministry tools, we need to make sure, like everything else that we do, that they are being developed only to glorify God and not just keeping us busy to shore up the foundations of our church.

God is our foundation; He is a sure foundation and He is the one who will bring others to the church as long as we are grounded in Him and Him alone.

76

Secrets

It appears that I have misjudged the world again. There was a letter in the newspaper, thanking an anonymous person, who paid a "lay-by" for a deserving family. As I rejoiced in the Christmas Spirit being alive and well, I prayed that the person's joy would not be spoilt. How could that happen? I hear you ask.

There was a time when for us money was very short. Farming was paying very little and neither of us had off-farm employment. One day I had a call. Someone had left some money to be given to a needy family and we had been brought to the benefactor's attention. I was told that the conditions were that no names were to be mentioned. I tried to think of some other family who would be more deserving. However, I accepted with good grace and rejoiced in the blessings that God had shown us.

A few days later, a lady I knew asked if I had received the call and proceeded to inform me that they had been the person who had recommended us. Oddly enough, it was this family that I almost recommended myself. I was very surprised at just how deflated I felt after learning this. The passage that came to mind was Matthew 6:1-4, which ends with: "Then your Father, who sees what is done in secret, will reward you." I realised that God not only rewarded those who give in secret but there is an immediate blessing enjoyed by those who receive. That blessing is spoilt when the secret no longer exists. My lesson was learnt, if you do something in secret, keep the secret or you will spoil the blessing that comes with the act of kindness.

Sometimes keeping quiet is a good thing.

77

Sharing Christmas

It was another Christmas that did not feel like Christmas. It was getting tedious. During the week I had listened while men smiled, crediting their wives with all the gift shopping, wives saying they were depressed because they had been left with all the work. I saw very few shops with decorations in place. To cap off the whole week, members of my own family wanted plans changed at the last minute to suit themselves. "God, why is Christmas such a chore?" I prayed.

Then, I saw the most common picture associated with Christmas. It was Joseph walking all the way to Bethlehem. He was sharing the workload!

If we are to believe the romantic stories of Christmas' past, all the members of the family worked together, to make sure everyone else in the family was cared for. I thought back to the many Christmas experiences I had as a child. The memories included all the adults working together. The men helped each other get the outside chores done, the women chatted, while they prepared the meals, as the children played together outside.

The birth of Jesus would not have happened, without the "Trinity" working together. "For God so loved the world that He gave His one and only Son, that whoever believes in Him shall not perish but have eternal life." (John 3:16). Christmas presents the greatest opportunity to tell the politically correct world about the love of Jesus. Yet, it seems to me, that we could easily let the opportunity slip through our fingers.

Yes, if God allows it, we will get another opportunity next year. Let's start planning now to share the greatest story ever by working together.

78

Shortcuts

There was a very long and difficult period in my life. During this time, I asked many of my Christian friends for prayer and support. This was given and appreciated; however, there were many people who thought that I should take steps of my own to fix the situation. It was even suggested that I could walk away from the problem.

I know that there are plenty of situations where Christians have to walk away, run even. After all, when Herod sought to kill Jesus, God told Joseph to take Mary and the Baby and escape to Egypt. (Matthew 2:13).

There were four things that God used to help me carry on. Firstly, there were the assurances that He gave me before I started. Secondly, there were the stories of David and Saul. David had refused to kill Saul on two separate occasions when God had handed him the opportunities. (1 Samuel 24:1-13 and 26:1-25). Thirdly, I had a vision of standing before God, on Judgement Day, and hearing Him say, "You know I had the answer, you just had to last three more days - you missed it by that much." Lastly, God sent me a non-church attending Christian who said, "If the Holy Spirit is telling you not to walk away, then DON'T."

God did eventually answer my prayers. Through those struggles, He taught me so much, most importantly that we must be very careful while supporting others. It is very easy to get discouraged about the length of time that God takes to answer some prayers, but we must not suggest, to others or ourselves, that a shortcut is acceptable.

Jude 17:20-25 is important, especially where it says: "Keep yourselves in God's love as you wait for the mercy of our Lord Jesus Christ..."

79

Signs

Things seemed to be on hold for such a long time and so I often felt like asking God for a sign. I wanted to know what I had to do to move forward. I wanted to know if I was getting in His road. I wanted to know how long it was going to be before something happened.

Each time that I felt like asking God for the sign I would remember another lady and the lesson she taught me about asking God for signs. Her life, at the time, was on hold while they waited for a property sale to go through and the move to their new place. There just seemed to be one hold up after another and so she asked God for a sign. She wanted to know how long it would be before they were able to move into the new place. One day while they were driving home, she looked up at the sky through the car window; there was a cloud that caught her attention. It was shaped like a very old-fashioned number four. No one else in the car knew what the significance of this would be as they had no idea of her prayer or how she wrote her fours. Now she still had a problem; was God telling her that they would be moving in four days; four weeks; four months; or even four years. She realised that even though God had given her a sign she didn't know much more than before.

Many people asked Jesus for signs while He walked on earth but He spoke to Thomas, who wanted signs, thus the name "Doubting Thomas" saying: "Thomas, because thou hast seen me thou hast believed, blessed are they that have not seen, and yet have believed." John 20:29.

80

Sinners Even

I walked up the steps leading to a church when a friend said, "Oh look, they'll let anyone in here." I gave them a good-natured dig in the ribs and replied: "Yeah, sinners even." We both knew why we were saying these things. We had both been involved with churches where you had to have certain qualities to be accepted. We both believe that churches are places for teaching all of us the most important things that God wants us to learn.

Where are they going to hear?

- That everyone is a sinner! (Romans 3:23)

- What sin is! That sin is not just murder or robbery but something as simple as just ignoring God. (Matthew 25:31-46)

- Where do they find out that the wages of sin is death? (Romans 6:23)

- Where will they learn that Hell is a real place, of darkness and evil? (Matthew 8:12)

- Where are they going to discover that Jesus loved us enough to come to earth? (John 3:16)

- How will they ever know that Jesus' death on the cross means that we can have our sins forgiven? (John 3:14-15)

- How will they be able to realise that when they ask Jesus for forgiveness He will be faithful and forgive us and as a result, we can gain eternal life in heaven? (1 John 1:9)

- When will they hear that Jesus will return one day? (1 Thessalonians 4:16-17)

If we cannot hear these things in a church, where else would you expect those in great need to hear them? Like Paul says: "How then shall they call on Him in whom they have not believed? And how shall they believe in Him of whom they have not heard? And how shall they hear without a preacher? And how shall they preach, except they be sent? As it is written, "How beautiful are the feet of them that preach the gospel of peace and bring glad tidings of good things." (Romans 10:14-15).

81

Standing Up

I remember a time when the children were very young. Life was lonely and my days were very long. One morning I got out of bed and said to the Lord, "I won't be able to stand it if I have no visitors today." My day progressed in the usual manner, tending the children's needs, washing clothes, cooking meals and general housework. My husband came home, we had tea, he went to make the numerous phone calls that went with his job and I put the children to bed. Walking back down the hall to do the dishes, I experienced what almost felt like a tap on the shoulder, a voice said. "Look you are still standing, walking even." What a sense of humour our God has! Here He was teaching me that even when I think I cannot go on; He knows that I can. He knows this because He made me, and He gave me skills and gifts that I have to use. There is no point telling Him I cannot go on because, even when I think I have exhausted the resources that He has given me, He will always be there to give me more.

Just as God told Moses, that He would teach him what to do, (Exodus 4:15) so will He teach us what He wants us to learn. While it is very easy to complain about what God might want you to do, just like children complain when parents ask them to do things, God wants us to learn that He will never ask us to do more than He is willing to help us do. In Philippians 4:13 Paul tells the church members at Philippi that he can do everything through God who gives him strength.

God will do the same for us.

82

Stay Out, Cat!

We are looking after a cat, and yes in its previous abode it was allowed to stay inside, in fact I'm pretty sure that its whole existence was inside. Several times a day, I have to remind this visiting moggy that it needs to stay outside. After an unusual number of extra reminders one day I found myself getting impatient. But...

God had a message for me. How many times does He have to stop me from going into places that He doesn't want me to go? I am again reminded and thankful for the fact that He is more patient with me than I was with the cat.

As we travel along our earthly road, God will have different plans for each stage of our lives. Just like our visiting cat, while he was once allowed inside, at this stage of his life he is not allowed and yet there will be a time when he will be able to enjoy the comforts of the indoors again no doubt, if he lives long enough.

There have been many times in my life when I have wanted to do certain things and yet God has clearly told me to stay out.

Psalm 139:23-24 says, "Search me O God and know my heart, try me, and know my thoughts; and see if there be any wicked way in me, lead me in the way everlasting." Again, in Proverbs 3:5-7, I read, "Trust in the Lord with all thine heart and lean not unto thine own understand. In all thy ways acknowledge Him and He shall direct thy paths. Be not wise in thine own eyes, fear the Lord, and depart from evil."

Yes, God sometimes says "stay out", but He knows best, and I'd rather stay out of something here on earth for a little while than out of Heaven forever.

83

Stewing

It was a very full day, I had two meetings and a dinner function. As I observed the people at each of these gatherings, I noticed that some were very upset with other members of the various groups. There were a lot of 'sour grapes' as they say. I wondered what it was that made the difference between these people and those that just got on with life. It would be ridiculous to assume that others had never been hurt or upset. One thing I did observe was that those who apparently spent a lot of time on their own were the ones who seemed unable to be nice, the ones most upset. Those who remained calm would appear to have other people to talk to and would get a better or different perspective.

So, what about those who spent a lot of time alone and still seemed to be able to stay calm in the face of such distress? My conclusion was that it was a matter of who they talked to while they were alone. For example, if I have something that is upsetting me and I am being sensible, it is God that I talk to, not myself. When I stew on my own, issues get blown out of proportion. I proved that myself in the week leading up to one particular function. Looking back, I realised that I had lost a lot of sleep simply because I hadn't constantly talked to God.

Philippians 4:8 says, "Finally, brethren whatsoever things are true, whatsoever things are honest, whatsoever things are just, whatsoever things are pure, whatsoever things are lovely, whatsoever things are of good report; if there be any virtue, and if there be any praise, think on these things."

Let's talk to God and stew sweet apples rather than sour grapes.

84

Such a small Thing

I shared a photo on the internet of a field of tulips in the Netherlands. One of my friends took exception and suggested that I check out a Tasmanian website. I did and discovered that there was just as big a field of tulips there. It was such a small thing to do, look closer to home.

Some weeks later I was thinking about this and I realised that we often do this in our Christian walk. We look in the obvious places to be missionaries, or give support, or preach. These are usually overseas in what we think are remote places. Sometimes, though, it is just a small thing to look closer to home.

My great grandfather, after he was converted, went to see a minister, declaring that he wanted to be a missionary and share the gospel. The minster's response was, "Sometimes God wants us to stay at home and share the gospel there." The story goes that my great grandfather refused to ever go on holidays after this. He didn't want to miss an opportunity to witness to someone in his hometown.

How do people get to hear about the gospel if there is no one to share it with them? Romans 10:14 reminds us, "How then shall they call on him in whom they have not believed? And how shall they believe in him of whom they have not heard? And how shall they hear without a preacher?" It is such a small thing to preach by setting a good example. Christ instructs us in Matthew 28:19-20, "Go ye therefore, and teach all nations... Teaching them to observe all things whatsoever I have commanded you," but let us not forget the nation that is right on our doorstep - HOME.

85

Tackling Goliath

I become aware of a problem that a particular church had. It was not the first time that I had heard about this problem. I was surprised, however, to find that it had resurfaced. This time the reaction of church members to this issue seemed to have them milling around and walking away. While those who were walking away had very Godly and good reasons to do so, I was aware that not everyone would be able and some would not want, to walk away.

Praying, early one morning, I realised that what the church was dealing with, was a very real problem but it was only a form of Goliath. God had to remind me that no problem is bigger than Goliath. I t was up to us to decide if we were going to sit in Saul's chair of fear or stand in David's sandals of faith. He also reminded me that there were times when I had faced my own Goliaths and I had quaked at the sound of their voices. Unlike David, I needed people to stand with me and help me. God had been gracious sending many people to stand alongside me, which they had faithfully done.

Regardless of where we live and what we do, there will always be a Goliath looming somewhere. Do we take God at His word or do we become dismayed and terrified (1 Samuel 17:11) just as the Israelites' army did?

Hopefully, we will take David's word to Goliath, "You come against me with sword and spear and javelin, but I come against you in the name of the Lord Almighty, the God of the armies of Israel, whom you have defied. This day the Lord will hand you over to me,..." (1 Samuel 17:45-46a).

86

Teaching and Learning

I was watching a re-run of a TV program in which a father discusses with his daughter his concern that he may not have taught her properly as she is behaving badly. Her response was, "You taught me properly, I just haven't learnt yet". I know so many parents have these thoughts over and over again during the trials of raising children.

I also realised the truth of the girl's statement. We can teach but we cannot make people learn. God teaches us but He won't force us to learn. I have seen many Christians with great passion try to teach people with the misguided premise that they would enter into the Kingdom of God. Unfortunately, they just end up getting frustrated because unless the Holy Spirit is working in the lives of those we are witnessing to there is no way that they are going to learn what we are trying to teach them. You cannot round up people like a herd of cows and force them into God's Kingdom. God will lead them, the Holy Spirit will teach them, and all we have to do is tell them what God wants them to know.

Even the disciples came and asked Jesus why he spoke in parables (Matthew 13:10) Jesus responded by saying, "Because it is given unto you to know the mysteries of the kingdom of heaven, but to them it is not given." (Matthew 13:11) and in verse 16 He says, "But blessed are your eyes for they see: and your ears, for they hear."

Christ wants us to teach, preach and lead all the people that we come in contact with, particularly our families, but it is the work of the Holy Spirit that will ultimately help people to learn.

87

Tell me the Old, Old Story

A few weeks ago, and again last Sunday we sang the hymn "Tell Me the Old, Old Story" and it got me thinking. I have been so very blessed because this is exactly what my mother and father have done for me. Over and over again they have shared about the times when God has used them, protected them, and most importantly they have told me how Jesus died for my sins and how through the power of the Holy Spirit I can carry out the plan that He has for me. My mother has a photographic memory and knows her scripture well and can constantly quote appropriate verses to me when I ring her with problems or in times of stress. She is a source of knowledge that I am ashamed to admit I don't have and very much aware that one day I will need to memorise Scriptures myself.

Those who know my mother know her as a very quiet, godly woman and to me as a child she was the perfect example of what a Christian woman was meant to be. So, it would be no surprise to imagine that I wanted to be exactly like her. However, as I saw it there was just one problem – I had too much of my father in me to ever be remotely like my mother. I prayed so many times during my childhood for God to make me like my mother and I struggled to follow her example. A bit like the story mum used to tell about a little girl with brown eyes praying for God to make them blue, until she grew up and went to Africa as a missionary and all the children had brown eyes and she realised that God had a very good reason for her to have brown eyes.

It has only been as I have grown older and travelled part of the path that God has mapped out for me that I have realised just how much God knew that I would need those qualities that were part of my father to get me through my journey in life. God knows what He has planned for me and He has made me the way I am for that very purpose and He made me from the only two people in this world that would help Him by being who they are and telling me that Old, Old story over and over again.

88

To the Congregation

Dear Fellow Christians,

I wanted to write and thank you for the fellowship we shared last weekend. I enjoyed our time together and saw again the hand of God in my own personal life.

From the safety of where I live, I have admired the tenacity of your community to keep going, not only through the floods that you have experienced but also preceding years of drought. You are a congregation with a heavy burden for the community in which you work and live. There is, as you rightly pointed out, a great need for people to understand not only His love for them but His desire for them to experience His plan of salvation and healing.

While we are the only hands that God has to use and the only mouths that God has to speak with, I am reminded of Moses and Aaron in Numbers 20:1-13 and how they were told by God to speak to the rock that was to give life-giving water to the Israelites. Instead, Moses struck the rock twice with his staff. It is easy to forget that we also sin when we don't trust God enough and add to His instructions. It was his lack of trust that Moses was punished for.

It is very easy to think sometimes that we are the only things that God can use. God is greater than all our hands, mouths, feet, and the entire church body. He will do amazing things in your community as long as you rest in Him. "For my yoke is easy and my burden is light", Matthew 11:30. As I remember that weekend, I pray that you will find again our amazing God of power.

89

Today We Remember – Good Friday

In Luke 23:35 we read, "And the people stood beholding, and the rulers also with them derided him, saying, He saved others, let him save himself, if he be Christ, the chosen of God." I was thinking about this verse last night and I even contemplated the idea: "well He was the Son of God, of course, He could have gotten Himself down off the cross and put Himself back up there just to prove that it could be done."

The next thought was "No, He could not have". Why? Because the minute He came down off the cross, He would have lost the one thing that made Him the perfect sacrifice for our sins. That one selfish act (sin) just to prove that He could do something that the mockers were taunting Him about, would have meant that He was no longer perfect. He would not have even been able to get back up on the cross because He would have become a sinner as well.

So, Jesus stayed there, in agony, not because He didn't have the power to come down, but because if He had, He would not have been able to defeat the devil, we would not have been able to come to Him as our Saviour and His sacrifice would not have been acceptable to God. How strong and pure was the love for us that kept Him there!

John 3:17-18 clearly states, "For God sent not his Son into the world to condemn the world; but that the world through him might be saved. He that believeth on him is not condemned but he that believeth not is condemned already, because he hath not believed in the name of the only begotten Son of God."

Yes, today we remember that Christ died for all of us because He loved us so much.

90

Touched by an Angel

I don't always like some people that I meet. One such person was diagnosed with terminal cancer. When the diagnosis was announced, I knew what they thought about God and where they would be spending eternity. I prayed honestly, "Lord, you know how I feel and I know you don't even want this person to spend their eternity in hell, but I cannot talk to this person, I can only pray for them." And pray I did.

After about three months, I came home one day, around lunchtime; feeling so tired I lay down in front of the television and watched a program with a Christian message called, "Touched by an Angel". The message, on this particular day, seemed to be extremely relevant to this person. I literally called out to them, over the miles that separated us, willing them to hear this message.

Two days later we were informed that their eternal journey had started. The next few days were filled with duties that come with assisting with funeral arrangements, and I forgot all about the television program.

The day after the funeral, I was driving into town, talking to God the way I do. "Well Lord, their choice has been made now; there is nothing more that can be done." Clearly, as if someone had spoken to me, a thought came to me, "Well there was that 'Touched by an Angel' program the other day." My response was just as simple: "Ok Lord, I leave it with you"

James 5:15 says, "And the prayer of faith shall save the sick, and the Lord shall raise him up and if he have committed sins, they shall be forgiven him."

In faith, I wait to see the outcome when I get to Heaven.

91

Umbrellas

When I hear the words, "Let's formalise things" in the business world I have confidence that things are being done correctly, however, when I hear these words in church all I think is, "Oh no here comes the big black umbrella again." Why? "What does an umbrella do?" It gives us shade from the sun and protection from rain. In hot or bad weather this is good but at church, the formalisation of any ministry or outreach to the world can also act as an umbrella. It shades us from God's Son, Jesus Christ and protects us from the showers of blessings that could be a result of our work.

I am not suggesting that Churches fall into the depths of utter chaos. There does need to be some form of structure but there are times, I feel, when formalisation is done in order to keep people in line with a particular doctrinal thinking, rather than allowing each individual person to be a personal channel for Christ. We might be surprised by how differently the Holy Spirit can work through each person with less formalisation.

God says in Isaiah 55:8-9, "For my thoughts are not your thoughts, neither are your ways my ways, saith the Lord, for as the heavens are higher than the earth, so are my ways higher than your ways, and my thoughts than your thoughts." Then in verse eleven, it says, "So shall my word be that goeth forth out of my mouth; it shall not return unto me void but it shall accomplish that which I please, and it shall prosper in the thing whereto I sent it."

Do you really want to be protected from Jesus or the blessings that He sends? Let's put down some of our umbrellas and get wet!

92

Unwanted Gifts

There has been a lot of talk amongst our friends about the gifts of the Holy Spirit and the lack of evidence of His work. On one occasion I was listening to someone preach about how the Holy Spirit hadn't been working in our lives and I got really mad. In my thoughts I screamed at God saying, "Will you please show this man how you have been working in my life all these years", and straight away God said "It's none of his business. What the Holy Spirit does through you is between you and Me."

The Bible describes the Holy Spirit as a comforter. (John 14:26) "But the comforter, which is the Holy Ghost, whom the Father will send in my name,..." He is not a "show off", He quietly comes into people's lives and shows them what to do and then gives them the strength to do it. There is very rarely any fanfare to announce what He is up to.

We are all given very different gifts by the Holy Spirit and some of them are not desirable in certain circumstances. I, myself once had what I considered to be a particular gift, yet it caused so much trouble between myself and a young Christian that I begged God to take it from me, which He did.

We as Christians cannot tell others what gifts they should or shouldn't have. That is God's privilege and right and to say that someone else should have what we have or don't have is legalistic and ultimately saying that God is wrong. Romans 12:6 says, "Having then gifts differing according to the grace that is given to us."

The gifts I have are between myself and God and I pray that He will use them for His glory only.

93

Value for Pain

While I realize that I am extremely blessed, there were definitely times when I argued that I wasn't. I was thinking about some of the things that had happened in my life. In particular, I was thinking about how I moved from house to house for a large part of my life, and how there appeared to be only one valuable lesson to come from that. I caught myself thinking that maybe I should have got a lot more lessons out of such an unpleasant experience. Some of this thinking also sprang from the fact that I had been knocking my body around trying to clean up an overgrown garden, asking myself quite a few times if the pain was worth the outcome.

The next question is, I guess, did God get value for pain. "For God so loved the world that he gave His one and only Son, for whoever believes in Him shall not perish but have eternal life." (John 3:16). I would imagine that if we gave up a son or daughter for a group of people, we would expect that all those people would be grateful at least, but more than likely we would expect that they would be indebted to us for life. What was the human response instead? Yes, some people are very grateful, serving their Lord and Saviour for their whole lives. Others, however, just ignore both God and His Son, some even go to the trouble to try and kill their only way out of hell.

Looking at the parable of the man who purchases a field to gain a pearl of great value (Matthew 13:44-46) I know that not everyone gets value for pain. And I pray that God will remind me that some rewards require a great deal of pain.

94

Visitors

A friend shared their frustration over her child's messy bedroom on Facebook and even showed her friends a photo. They got lots of support and advice from their Facebook friends. Reading through the comments it made me realise that Facebook is the Twenty-First Century's visiting routine. In times past, people would actually knock on your door and you could invite them in. These days by posting your status and photos, you invite people into your life. It's a lot more controlled, in that they only get to see what you want them to see. The variety of people who get invited is greater but that also means that there is a greater diversity of advice, good or bad.

As I thought about this later, I was reminded about the visitors who would actually come to my home as a newlywed housewife. It seemed to me that it would be the one day that I had decided not to make the bed or do the washing up, that there would be a knock on the door. One particular young visitor would delight in checking out the house and reporting to the adults exactly what hadn't been done that day. It always felt a bit like judgement day.

If I had been wiser or more spiritually mature, I'm sure that I would have taken Proverbs 27:1 to heart. "Boast not thyself of tomorrow for thou knowest not what a day may bring forth." If I had I would have made sure that I did those jobs every day.

In the same way, as I didn't know when this visitor would call, I don't know when Jesus is going to knock on my life's door. He will be calling me to check out my life's work, not my housework. Are you ready to have your life's work checked?

95

Waiting on Him

As I watched the animals in the midst of a drought, I didn't see them rushing around getting in a flap. They were calmly getting on with life and resting in the knowledge that someone would look after them. They knew that feed was short, and things were tough! They could not however even ask the farmer if he is going to look after them to get reassurance that they would have a meal each day. Even if the farmer could tell them every day that he would look after them, they were unable to understand. They just trusted that things would happen, blindly maybe, but they still trusted.

God gives us reassurance, of His care, in black and white, not just once but over and over again when we read His word. Yet many of us struggle to trust Him. Listen to what He says today. "Rest in the Lord, and wait patiently for Him: fret not thyself because of him who prospereth in his way, because of the man who bringeth wicked devices to pass." Psalm 37:7.

There are so many times in my life when I still find it hard to trust God, to believe with both my head and my heart that He is in control. This happens most often when I am asked by God to wait for Him. Wait for His time! It is such a hard thing for me to do because I am a person of action. I am surprised as I study my Bible just how many verses there are that tell me to wait. As I practice trusting Him each day then one day, I will be able to quote Lamentations 3:26 confidently, "It is good that a man should both hope and quietly wait for the Salvation of the Lord."

96

Weeding

I decided to do some weeding in my front garden. I started at the garden edge and pulled grass out around some very strongly grounded plants. I then moved further into the garden. Suddenly there was a fairly large plant in amongst the weeds. It had looked like a mature plant that should have been very firmly rooted in the soil, but it wasn't. I then came across a patch of self-sown seedlings and realised that if I was not careful, I could easily destroy them.

We are like these plants in my garden. Some are strongly rooted in the soil with a network of support. Some look as if they are mature plants but their root system is fragile, leaving it vulnerable to attacks. Some people are just like those seedlings, weak and delicate. When we try to help others, we have no idea which category they are going to fall into. We must be very careful to ask God how He wants us to proceed.

It surprised me as I weeded around the seedlings carefully, how many times my hand stopped short of a seedling. It had nothing to do with me being able to clearly see what I was doing, as there was another plant as well as my hair constantly falling down over my eyes, obscuring my vision.

1 Corinthians 13:1-2 says, "Though I speak with the tongues of men and of angels, and have not charity, I am become as sounding brass, or a tinkling cymbal. And though I have the gift of prophecy and understand all mysteries and all knowledge; and though I have all faith, so that I could remove mountains and have not charity, I am nothing."

It is good to share our love for God but let us do it carefully, prayerfully and with love!

97

What a Week

I have had a week which is in contrast to another week that I wrote about a few years ago. The previous one had been such a highlight of that year. This last week, (well its only half over at writing) has been such a struggle. First, I was laid low with a head that kept spinning; this meant that I had to opt out of a function that I was helping to organise. I spent a lot of time fretting about not being reliable because this lightheadedness comes at such random times and I hate saying I will do something and then have to pull out at the last minute. I worried if I should resign from a couple of volunteer positions I am already doing. I turned down an opportunity to fill in for a Scripture Teacher because I was just so unsure that I could be relied on to be there.

My emotions swung between wanting to come out fighting to wanting to crawl into a hole in the side of a riverbank and stay there.

To add to my grief, the water jacket in my stove sprang a leak, squirting water all over the kitchen floor. Turning off the taps at the hot water tank didn't stem the flow. The plumber was very busy, so we knew this was not going to an easy fix. As I sat, watching my washing flapping in the stiff breeze on the first sunny day I had seen since I had fallen sick, I asked God, "What are you trying to teach me? Where do you want me to go? Where is my message?"

There was this nagging thought in the back of mind, which was telling me that God has big plans for me and if I could see it all from here it would scare me silly. Some people had suggested that I should allow God to guide me. So, I decided to start there. There were six references under the word "guide" so I started with the one in John's gospel, one of my favourite books in the bible.

Starting with Verse 12 through to verse 14, I read: "I have yet many things to say unto you but ye cannot bear them now. Howbeit when he, the spirit of truth is come, he will guide you into all truth: for he shall not speak of himself; but whatsoever he shall hear, that shall he speak; and He will shew you things to come. He shall glorify me for He shall receive of mine and shall shew it unto you."

So, I wait!

98

What's in a Name

It was another frustrating morning. I hung out the washing, which had streaks of dust marks all over the clothes. I thought I hate my washing machine; I would not recommend this brand of machine to anyone. In fact, I was tempted to get on Facebook and blast the company for making my life so difficult. If you are buying some new piece of equipment, it is common practice to ask others what brand they would recommend. It did get me thinking though about "Names". Why did we buy this particular brand? Previous machines of this brand had proved to be very effective in delivering clean washing over and over again. I was thinking about a shopping trip recently where my daughter and I went into a "Reject Shop" and I spotted my favourite "Dove" brand body wash at a cheaper price than I would normally pay at my local supermarket. I was reluctant to buy it there because the name "Reject" implies that stock has been rejected. Has it been rejected for substandard quality? Even when my head said "no", my heart said "maybe". My thoughts then moved to my regular supermarket, where I purchase many of my food products because they meet my dietary needs at a low price. Would I recommend them to others? Not really because I have issues with the way they do business. If you are buying some new piece of equipment, it is common practice to ask others what brand they would recommend.

So, what about how people react to the name of "Jesus". Do they react badly because of the way they see people behave? If people see Christians behaving badly, do they see Jesus as someone who will not keep His promises? We are called to be witnesses for Jesus and by being faithful we are the people who tell the rest of the world about Jesus and how much He loves them. In John 13:34-35 Jesus says "A new commandment I give unto you, that ye also love one another as I have loved you. By this shall all men know that ye are my disciples if ye have love one to another." When we do this, we will be recommending Jesus not as a Name but as the Saviour of the World.

99

When God says "No"

During a conversation about answered prayer, a comment was made like, "Don't be surprised if God says no." As I thought about this the next day my train of thoughts went something like this. See if you can follow it with me?

When God says "NO" He does so because He has our best interests at heart. We would say "No" to our children if they wanted something that would harm them. When I give in to my children, they have a habit of saying, "Thank you, I love you". My response lately has been, "Say that when I say 'No' please." Oh dear, don't I do the same thing to God? What is my response to God when He says "NO" to me?

It is still very easy to expect God to say "Yes" to all that we ask of Him. In fact, we can be accused of a lack of faith if we don't get a Yes answer. Sometimes God knows that if He said "yes" to some of our requests, we would not depend on Him for His strength, courage, and our faith in Him would not be built up in the way that He knows it should be.

Moses asked to see the face of God and God said "No". (Exodus 33:20). Moses pleaded with God to let him go into the Promised Land and God said: "No". (Deuteronomy 3:23-27). David pleaded for the life of his child and God said "No" (2 Samuel 12:15-18). God refuses to answer the prayers of a rebellious Israel (Ezekiel 20:3). Paul had to accept that God would not answer his prayer for good health. (2 Corinthians 12:8).

Next time God says "No" to me, hopefully, before I get miserable, I will remember that God knows best.

100

Which Destination

A friend was struggling with how long it was taking for a project to get finished. At the same time, I was struggling with how long it was taking for me to get a new project underway. We both had different destinations, but we weren't getting there very fast. As I prayed and thought about this it occurred to me, that it's not the destination but what we learn during the journey that really counts. After all, I have a teaching degree that I never seem to use in the traditional sense and I often ask God why He made me do it. The answer every time is, "It's what you learnt during the process that was important to Me, not the degree."

Having decided that the journey was the important thing, not the destination, my next thought was: "No hang on, there is one destination that does matter, our eternal destination." So, am I wrong? No! Here on earth, it is the journey that counts, not the many destinations. After all, there are many destinations during our lives. First, we have to reach toddlerhood, then childhood, independence and finally adulthood. Other destinations are Kindergarten, Primary and High School, University and our first job. There is for many of us marriage, children, mortgage etc but not necessarily in the same order and some of these will not be part of our lives anyway. For each of us, our journeys will be different, take varying lengths of time to reach and each of us will have to meet and overcome many diverse challenges to make progress.

Hebrews 12:1-2 tells me "Wherefore seeing we also are compassed about with so great a cloud of witnesses, let us lay aside every weight (in my case doubt and frustration) and the sin which doth so easily beset us and let us run with patience the race that is set before us. Looking unto Jesus the author and finisher of our faith: who for the joy that was set before him endured the cross, despising the shame and is set down at the right hand of the throne of God."

Our eternal destination is either Heaven or hell and that also depends on what we learn while we are here on earth.

Other Books by this Author

All these books are available as eBooks

Turning Water into Wine 2nd Edition
100 Stories of God's Hand in Life

Still More Water into Wine
100 Stories of God's Hand in Life

365 Glasses of Wine Revised Edition
Short Devotionals for each day of the year

Reflections Revision Edition
Australian Stories from my Father's Past

Conversations with Myself – Volume 1 2nd Edition
100 Stories of Hope, Faith and Determination

Whispers from on High
Poems and short stories

Follow Helen Brown on:

Facebook: https://www.facebook.com/HelenBrownCollection/

Instagram: https://www.instagram.com/helen_brown_books/

Pinterest: https://www.pinterest.com.au/helenbrown58726/

www.ingramcontent.com/pod-product-compliance
Lightning Source LLC
Chambersburg PA
CBHW030301010526
44107CB00053B/1770